''Broc Jerrel left an indelible imprint too, an imprint of superiority on the Hoosier hardboards. . . .

His amazing ability aligned with cocky confidence made him the most discussed, cussed and cheered player of his time. He was a 'Little Giant' to Bosse boosters, a 'Little Devil' and a 'Show Off' to others as he tantalized and taunted opponents with his wizardry. He was a Houdini, who could do everything with a basketball but pull a rabbit out of it and there were some sure he could do just that if the occasion demanded. . . .

Bryan 'Broc' Jerrel, the Basketball Brain, was the greatest of the high schoolers I saw play and I know that a vast majority of those who cussed and booed him would pick him first of all on a team that was to play for their life.''

Dan Scism, former Sports Editor, *The Evansville Courier* as quoted in *Hoopla* magazine, January 1971.

Frank Gilbasion

BROC

THE LITTLEST CHAMPION

The Basketball Saga of Bryan "Broc" Jerrel
and the Evansville Bosse Bulldogs

TIMOTHY BAIZE
1989

(Broc's nephew)
Evansville paper spelled my
name wrong & he copied it.
See chapters 11 & 12

Printed in the United States of America
by
Schutte Lithography, Inc.

Library of Congress Catalog Card Number: 89-92510
ISBN 0-9625193-0-8

Baize, Timothy, 1944—
Broc, the littlest champion
1. Jerrel, Bryan. 2. Basketball players—Indiana—Biography. 3. Basketball—Indiana—History. I. Title.
796.32′3′0924[B] 89-92510
ISBN 0-9625193-0-8

Timothy Baize
Evansville, IN 47711

Dedicated to the memory of my grandmother,
Mommy, and to the most precious parts of my life,
my wife Terry and my children, Hajja and Jonah

BROC
THE LITTLEST CHAMPION
OF
INDIANA HIGH SCHOOL
BASKETBALL

TABLE OF CONTENTS

PART V

PART VI

PART VII

PART VIII

ACKNOWLEDGEMENTS

I am grateful to all who contributed material to this book. In particular, I thank my friend, Bill Wiist, who was virtually the first to read and like the finished manuscript. I needed the approval.

Also my colleague Norm Kniese reviewed a portion of it.

My father-in-law, Allen Goebel, entertained himself perusing the manuscript.

My mother-in-law, Gwen Goebel, encouraged and supported me.

Dr. Virginia Grabill, my college mentor, very graciously agreed to proofread every word. A tremendously capable woman, she taught me to think about what I write.

My father, Adrian Baize, gave it his seal of approval.

The manuscript was typed by my dear cousin Martha Todrank, who was ever patient and diligent.

My appreciation goes to good friend and colleague, Bob Hammonds, media specialist extraordinaire at Evansville's Reitz High School for his expertise and assistance.

Throughout this writing and publishing venture, I have greatly appreciated the support, sacrifice, and love of my wife, Terry, who laughed out loud as she read.

I am indebted to Betty Lou Jerrel, Broc's wife, for advice and assistance.

I thank all my friends who encouraged and supported me through this endeavor.

Indeed, I thank Broc and the Bosse Bulldogs for their undeniable greatness.

And, finally, thank you, Lord, for making all things possible.

INTRODUCTION

In the Hoosier state, basketball is Indiana's game. There are probably more basketball goals per capita than any other state. And rightly so! In fact, Governor Evan Bayh ordered one erected in the driveway of the Executive Mansion in Indianapolis.

Formerly, another book and movie called *Hoosiers* touted Indiana basketball. It celebrated the courage, the greatness, the spirit that can come from even a tiny, rural school. But, this book is *Broc The Littlest Champion*. It too celebrates an underdog—a diminutive 5-7 court master.

Broc is the dazzling dynamo who out-dribbles, out-maneuvers, out-smarts nearly all competition. In sickness and in health, when Broc and pivotman Bud take on contenders, the show is on the hardwood. On the court Broc is the wiz, the mighty mite, the tactician with laser-like agility.

This book too applauds Hoosier Hysteria—basketball. In 1944, the Evansville Bosse Bulldogs post a mediocre 9-7 regular season record mostly because of illness, injury, and destiny. They enter competition in the Indiana High School Athletic Association State Basketball Tournament as the Cinderella team—no chance in the world.

Although Broc was one of the most cussed, discussed, and loved players ever to pound the leather on Indiana hardwoods, many who saw him play would pick him first on a team that would play for their lives. One sportswriter called him the best basketball player under six feet.

In 1939, the inventor of basketball, Dr. James Naismith, wrote in *The Rotarian* magazine of the challenges of basketball:

> The more I watch the game, the more I realize that while easy to understand and simple to demonstrate, it is nevertheless a challenge to skill. It is only through thorough grounding in the fundamentals and constant practice that championships are won.

Dr. Naismith would have appreciated Broc's skill and what Broc did to advance the sport they both loved so deeply. Broc was instrumental in helping basketball make a quantum leap.

Hoosiers might have started the ball bouncing; *Broc* scoops it up, dribbles, passes, and shoots it with the finesse of a Rembrandt.

Broc *is* the littlest champion.

Timothy Baize 1989

PART I

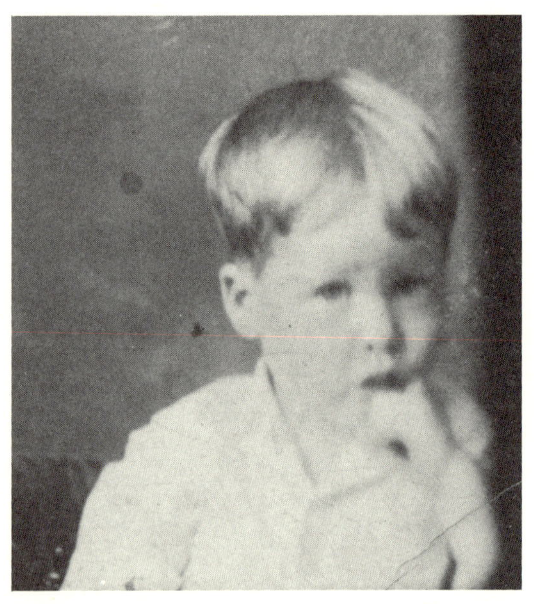

Broc, the littlest champion?

1

BROC AND THE BOYS BEGIN

Many who see *him* play basketball would pick *him* to play for their lives.

One sportswriter calls *him* "the Barrymore of the hardwood."

Ten years before Milan's Bobby Plump *(Hoosiers)* sinks the famed last second shot to defeat Muncie Central for the 1954 Indiana State Championship, *he* is dribbling zig zags around and shooting bombs over many of Hoosier high school basketball's best players.

And Carl Wiegman in his newspaper column places *him* beside "The Big O," Oscar Robertson, as guard on an all-time best five Indiana basketball team. But who is he?

He's as much a part of the rich Indiana basketball tradition as Isiah Thomas, Johnny Wooden,

Steve Alford, and Larry Bird. Unlike all these players, however, he is well under 6-0.

Affectionately, I call him Uncle Broc, but his full name is Bryan "Broc" Jerrel. At 5-7 he is probably the least identifiable but nevertheless an extraordinary hoopster. As a high school junior, he is head and shoulders above competitors though shorter than any of them. In fact, early in his career he is often mistaken for the team mascot.

The littlest champion of Indiana high school basketball has no rival as he spearheads the Evansville Bosse Bulldogs to the Finals of the state basketball tournament during "March Madness," a part of Hoosier Basketball Hysteria in 1944. At the pinnacle of his high school career, one sportswriter calls him the best basketball player under six feet.

During basketball season in 1944, the epicenter of Indiana high school competition is the Evansville Bosse Bulldogs and the shock wave Bryan "Broc" Jerrel.

This book spins the true saga of a team and its star who vie for the state championship against innumerable odds. Led by Bryan "Broc" Jerrel, the Evansville Bosse Bulldogs begin their ascent to the Indiana basketball crown in February 1944 against 777 prep schools.

Yet, Grandpa (Broc's father Rush), Broc, and several of his teammates actually conceive winning the state championship while pupils in elementary school in 1936. Every year thereafter, Grandpa drives Broc and any boys who will go to the State Championship at Indianapolis' Butler Fieldhouse.

In fact, in 1938, for the second consecutive year, Broc's father Rush (Grandpa), a railway mail clerk, shepherds Broc and his school mates to Indianapolis' Butler Fieldhouse to experience first hand the echos, the sense, the enormity of a 15,000 seat stadium. Grandpa puts the boys up in rented rooms along Meridian Street near the fieldhouse. Donning black gym shoes, shooting at netless hoops, the lads ease into the mammoth facility where, the day before, they watched Fort Wayne South eek out a two-point victory over Hammond Central. The youngsters return to Evansville with visions of basketball championships bouncing in their heads.

Four of the boys on that trip form the nucleus of a revolutionary cage quartet that would re-define Evansville and Indiana "round ball." One "carrot-topped" lad would emerge as an undisputed magician with the basketball, the Houdini of Hoosier hardwood—Bryan "Broc" Jerrel.

Julius "Bud" Ritter, Norm McCool, Erwin "Podjo" Scholz, and Broc comprise the formidable foursome. Broc is the leader, the genius, the champion. Sportswriters call him "The Brain" and "The Red-headed Spark Plug." After forty-two years as Sports Editor of *The Evansville Courier*, Dan Scism lauds Broc as "The most valuable high school basketball player I ever saw."

Although Broc's fame is now elusive—a dim screen in a film of memories—amidst the basketball hysteria of 1944 so many plaudits are heaped upon him that, at first, he seems undeserving. However, in his capacity as floor general for Bosse, he is heralded for his uncanny and unequaled game perception, his grace under pressure, his extraordinary dribbling and ball handling, his shooting, and his court savvy. He can do it all; amusingly, however, he is a poor leaper.

Once squeezed in by three opponents and an out-of-bound's line, Broc simply gestures "time-out" to the official; in 1944, few even imagined that option.

Broc's beginnings reveal a modest, middle class upbringing at 1315 Henning—just two blocks from Bosse High School. Living nearby at 1650 Kerth Avenue is Broc's best friend, Bud Ritter, who bicycles by each day to meet en route to school. And Norm McCool lives at 1355 Bayard Park Drive. Even closer at 1115 Henning is good friend Podjo Scholz who later attends Washington Elementary and Bosse High Schools with Broc and Bud. Since Broc's house offers the most central location of the four, everyone comes to his house.

As a youngster Broc dribbles on compacted dirt and shoots at a makeshift plywood backboard, nailed to a woodframed garage. Not a glamorous beginning! It's one of those backyard-to-Butler Fieldhouse stories: talented, young, ambitious lad learns game on garage goal, matures into extraordinary, remarkable basketball giant—but stands a mere 5-7.

The elder son of my grandparents Minnie and Rush Jerrel, Broc is born January 29, 1927. Very much a zealous sportsman, Grandpa instructs him early on. Not one to dillydally, Grandpa hands Broc a basketball; almost as soon as he waddles, he dribbles. He's been holding the ball longer than he has been able to babble his name. As Grandpa kindles Broc's enthusiasm for and prowess in the game, the little red-head dribbles, passes, and shoots with aplomb—all within Grandpa's scheme of instruction and development.

In the next step, Grandpa enlists a metal worker to fashion a three-eighths inch iron rod into a basketball hoop. Mounted about five feet up the basement wall, it's impossible to fix the number of rubber balls that bobble and rattle on, off, and through that cylinder. But by age seven Broc dribbles for hours as smaller brother Gene tries to guard him.

Then, one day at Grandpa's command Broc is blindfolded while dribbling; without visual cues, distractions, or stimuli, he perfects the controlled bouncing and movement of the ball and body in concert. Thus, his dribbling achieves a remarkable level. With painstaking practice he maneuvers his body, passes to teammates, dodges opposition, backs up, reads defenses, *and* dribbles the basketball—all without ever watching the ball.

Early on, Grandpa instills in Broc and several of the boys that basketball is a game more of skill than power. Thus, Broc's motions and floor movements are fluid-based not power-based.

Unfettered by the ball, he can concentrate on the game, on tactics, on winning. Further enhancing his dribbling skill, fully grown Broc stands only 5-7; from that height with knees bent, his dribble is appreciably lower (reducing the error margin), giving greater ball control and more immediate maneuverability. Simple physics!

Before moving to Washington School district in the sixth grade where he teams with McCool, Bud, and Broc, Podjo Scholz attends Stanley Hall with Jack Matthews. Four or so blocks from Broc's house, Podjo persuades Jack Matthews to knock the bottom out of a waste can and nail the cylinder to a basement wall. Hour after hour they toss a tennis ball into it. Two more team members begin carving their basketball destiny.

From a large but poor family, another young man starts his basketball career about 10-12 blocks north of Bosse High School. Gene Schmidt's beginnings are misfortunate. When he is twelve, his mother dies. As a result he must live with one of his three sisters six months at a time then live with another and so on. But through immense compassion, the Ritters invite Schmidt to live with them during the last part of the 1944 cage season. Accepted and loved, he remains there well after basketball ends.

His is a warm success story. Since he can remember, he visualizes starring on a basketball team. So after Coach Keller discovers him in his physical education class, he's on his way.

Schmidt gets his early basketball upbringing shooting a ball in rain, snow, or sleet into a peach basket in neighbor Marv Bates' backyard. Schmidt credits Bates with teaching him how to be competitive and with nurturing his early roundball talent. Destiny.

Matthews starts the 1944 season as guard opposite Broc; Schmidt starts forward; and Podjo sits on the bench, an able substitute when needed. Playing beside Broc, Matthews feels extremely confident and secure. "I knew if we ever got into a jam, Broc would get us out!" Matthews affirms. He knows Broc is the master, the star, and that makes Matthews feel good.

As Broc outgrows the basement goal, Grandpa enlists a fellow railroad postal worker to craft a backboard. Quite an amateur carpenter, Joe Alley cuts a sturdy backboard, nails it to two-by-fours that protrude three feet through the garage. Though the ground is dirt and pebbles, countless feet trample it, innumerable dribbles pound it day and night, in and out of season.

Goal and backboard endure no less. Even today the garage reveals plugged openings through which two-by-fours reached. Now, however, the house and neighbors are dumb to the sound of Broc and the boys dribbling, clonking, banging, and bobbling the basketball on that backyard goal.

Since his home is only four blocks from Washington Elementary School, Broc bicycles to school as do Bud Ritter, Podjo Scholz, and Norm McCool. There the quartet gains vital experience playing on the same squad. The early playing experience, however, comes in backyard play on that goal at the Jerrels.

While Bud, Broc, and the boys spend hours dribbling, shooting, faking at the Jerrels, Grandpa happily sits inside jawboning with "Big Jim" (Bud's older brother) about basketball technique, Grandpa's accomplishments, and his goal for the boys—the state championship. After almost every one of his questions or assertions, Grandpa seeks approval with "Isn't that right, Big Jim?" And, Big Jim always responds with "Yes, Sir!"

At the Jerrel household, the game is played inside as well as outside—and everybody is happy.

A few words about this Big Jim fellow. Almost as tall, Bud's brother James "Tiger" Ritter (Big Jim to Grandpa) is three years older than Bud. Very close, Tiger and Bud run around together but virtually have none of the customary sibling rivalry. In attendance at every high school game, Tiger is among the handful permitted in the Bulldog dressing room after each game. He's a loyal Bosse alumnus.

Since he is more mature, Tiger is an important influence on Bud, helping him "grow up"

In his backyard, the littlest champion strikes his best quarterback passing pose en route to Butler Fieldhouse.

faster than his peers. This growing up, coupled with Bud's varsity play as a freshman, of course, enables him to assume a team leadership role (Broc is captain) that is so crucial in clutch, pressure conditions the Bulldogs will face. Destiny.

Orphaned at age 3, Mommy (Broc's mother) loves family and friends and activity. So as the boys are playing ball at Washington and Bosse, they're in and out of the Jerrel house like a candy store. And Mommy relishes it. She cooks for anybody who's there—breakfast, lunch, dinner.

Her specialties include such *homemade* delights as waffles, noodles, mush, chili, vegetable soup, chicken and dumplings, applesauce with red hots, bread pudding, fudge, fresh-cut fried corn, fresh green beans with ham, navy beans with ham hock, and Broc's favorite macaroni and cheese. And the list is by no means exhaustive. Despite the "home cooking," the boys are virtually all thin as rails. But then they hustle.

In elementary school, the boys are so good in the third and fourth grades they play on the fifth grade team. From fifth to eighth grades they are undefeated. On one occasion against Stanley Hall Elementary, however, they are almost self-defeated. As it happens, teammate "Bulldog" Ewing dribbles past the ten-second line, pulls up in the corner, and launches four left-handed hook shots, all of which miss. Bud tells Broc if Bulldog tries to throw up another Bud will block it. Bulldog does; Bud blocks, passes it to Broc. They never again let Bulldog have the ball.

Destiny seems to be continually at work. Broc becomes master of another turf—the marble ring. In 1938, marble shooting is a popular pastime for boys. Perhaps as a diversion, Broc exhibits his prowess with a much tinier sphere—the marble.

Competitions abound in many Evansville elementary schools. As a sixth-grader, Broc is one of seventy competitors at Washington Elementary's marble shootout. Able to outshoot eighth grader Staley Henshaw, Broc captures the school championship and is hoisted on the shoulders of classmates who parade him around the school grounds amidst hoots and hollers.

The littlest champion is not only a basketball sharpshooter but also a crack *marble* shooter. His sphere of influence is extensive.

Nearly every Saturday in the seventh and eighth grades, Grandpa is granted permission to use the Washington School Gym to drill and scrimmage Broc and his teammates. During this period Broc develops the two-handed set shot; he performs it with such delicacy and aplomb from the top of the key and beyond that Matthews observes, "Broc seems to caress the ball ever so softly." Thus, the shot is very soft, highly arched, never banked; and the net pops from the perfect drop of the

Broc, becoming the littlest champion

slightly spinning ball—a three-pointer by today's standards.

It is from watching and studying Broc that Matthews develops his outside shooting techniques.

Grandpa successfully teaches the boys basketball basics, drills, strategy; Podjo even credits him with teaching him the game. But, when Grandpa can't get them into a gym, the Washington School custodian, an avid player, unlocks the door.

When they just can't gain legitimate access to a gym, Bud and Broc find an open window at Bosse or Washington. Although they trespass, they never vandalize. Coincidentally, Matthews and Podjo are also trying to get into any gym they can. But, when they try to climb into a Washington School window, Principal Carl Lemme discovers them and gives them a harsh verbal reprimand.

To watch the Evansville College Purple Aces play, Schmidt crawls in the bathroom window of the Indiana National Guard Armory near his home. But *he* is never caught.

Basketball is their passion.

When not climbing through windows, Podjo and Broc become part-time thespians at Washington in 1940. In their acting debut, they portray Huckleberry Finn and Tom Sawyer in a play of the same name. Thespians?

Despite their drama debut and the allure of Broadway and Hollywood, Podjo and Broc can't stay away from roundball. The same year, they "skip school" to attend a Sectional tournament

Broc (left) and Podjo (right) search for their next win while Bud (center) appears as if he's already found it.

game at Central Gym. Although they think they've got away with it, Principal Lemme uncovers the plot and identifies the guilty parties.

In his deep, authoritative tone, Mr. Lemme makes this request over the school's P.A. system: "Send Mr. Scholz and Mr. Jerrel to my office immediately!" For punishment they are given severe reprimands. It was difficult to fool Mr. Lemme (this writer knows from his own experience). Ironically, however, Grandpa might even have driven the boys to the game.

As the weather warms to late spring, Broc adds another accolade and championship to his repertory. Across from Bosse High School at a student hangout, Duncan YO-YO sponsors one of its frequent, popular, competitions. Broc survives the competition and takes home a vest sweater with a YO-YO emblem on it and a large Baby Ruth candy bar. Not exactly an all-expense paid trip to London, but he's only thirteen.

2

GREENIES, GRANDPA, GAME CLOCK, AND GROVE

Often Broc goes to any end to observe and study players; whenever a quality team competes at Central Gym, Broc and Bud are there to glean new techniques and styles. To gain entrance, they rattle the players' door on the side and are let in by a student manager. Never do they pay the usual fifteen cents for a bleacher seat. While other young boys watch comedies and serials at Washington Movie Theatre, Broc polishes dribbling and shooting and scrutinizes other prep players for hints to improve his game.

And it's during a neighborhood game that Broc acquires his name. Because of his bright red hair, kids call him "Bricky" and "Brocky." He even writes the latter on his school notebook. But, after a newspaper article erroneously prints "Broc" and fellow students address him as such, he adopts it because of its uniqueness, its different spelling, and its strong sound.

About the time he enters Bosse in early 1941, Grandpa and family move a few blocks to 1204 East Blackford, one half block from the school. The newly built one and one-half story (which this writer remembers) soon sports a goal in the backyard atop an elaborate two-by-four scaffold. Modeled after the goals at Butler Fieldhouse, it also protrudes to allow high speed lay-ups by players. And like the goal on the garage on Henning, Joe Alley is responsible for the construction. With only clay stretching several feet in front of it, Broc and the boys relentlessly play night and day. A lawn-mower isn't much needed.

When Bud and Broc do enter Bosse High School in January 1941 (students enter high school in September *and* January), half the freshman basketball season is completed, so they don't try out; it would be foolish to waste their eligibility on half a season. So, they are relegated to an organized practice in the girls' gym under senior player, Bob Million.

Ironically, Million drops them for not having varsity potential. So much for foresight! Thus, they play pickup games on Bosse's asphalt courts with varsity and reserve players. Although the smallest and youngest, Broc is normally the first player chosen by a team.

"Laddie," Grandpa, and 1204 East Blackford

Interestingly, during this first year at Bosse, Bud grows from 5-8 to 6-3. Although he will grow no taller, he is a coaches' dream.

Next fall 1941, however, and still freshmen, Bud and Broc try out for the team: Bud is put on the varsity coached by Harry King; Broc is put on the varsity-reserve with mentor Arad McCutchan who would coach Evansville College to five NCAA Division II Basketball Championships and be inducted into the exclusive National Basketball Hall of Fame. Not bad for two "greenies!" Bud and Broc now have four full years of playing eligibility.

As mentioned, Grandpa always wants to help the boys, to teach them the fundamentals of the game. Ahead of his time, he is often ridiculed for his techniques and instruction. But, Grandpa knows the game. For example, he teaches Broc the two-handed set shot which he executes after receiving the ball chin high. Since he is only 130 pounds, however, he must jump to power it. Grandpa demands he practice the shot endlessly; Broc does. Soon he hits almost flawlessly from near the ten-second line.

But, from inside the key, Broc puts up a one-handed shot for which he also leaves the floor. (Grandpa really wants all the boys to shoot the one-handed shot.)

Grandpa can go too far, however. A slender, broad-shouldered 5-10 and 165 pounds, he is a Damon Runyan figure, complete with unlighted cigar, overcoat, wide-brimmed hat; when not

Broc, the littlest champion, is maturing.

working, he attends every Bosse practice. Hooping, hollering, rooting, he is frequently encouraging, positive—a major influence on several team members. High on emotion, Grandpa makes a person competitive.

Grandpa is master of the colorful expression. Sometimes, he tells Broc "If I couldn't play any better than that I'd go down to the river and start walking till my hat started floating." Or, he boasts "I could walk up a plowed field with a piano on my back and play better than you!"

Broc is unshaken. "When I'm playing," Broc affirms, "I don't care who's there, how many, how loud, or anything." Grandpa was a very good player himself; Broc becomes extraordinary.

Making the varsity-reserve squad as a freshman is acceptable to Broc although the games are often only attended by parents, close relatives, friends, and godparents. But, when his talent develops and his fame spreads, he'll pack 'em in every gym the Bulldogs play.

But, one particularly agonizing dilemma occurs in mid-season play. Late in the fourth quarter, Broc hears a beverage vendor shout "Shoot! Shoot!" Without thinking, believing time would expire (Central Gym only had a clock and scoreboard at one end), he obediently turns goalward and lofts the ball at the backboard. Before falling to the hardwood, the ball ricochets off nearly every lamp, beam, and rafter atop Central Gym.

A glimpse of the game clock shows Broc one

and one-half minutes of official time remain. Broc fears this mental error will blacklist him with Coach McCutchan. "If you'll give me another chance, I'll show you I can play," Broc pleads.

Nodding approval, Mr. McCutchan assures Broc he will have ample time to prove himself.

That fateful shot proves an inexpensive but painful competitive sports lesson of which Broc is always mindful; he never again competes without ever present knowledge of the time clock.

Soon, another momentous instruction is afforded Broc. And with outstretched arms he accepts this one. During a rather lackluster season, Broc witnesses highly regarded Art Grove, Washington, Indiana High School guard, dribble behind his back in competition at Central Gym. Awed by Grove's performance, Broc immediately practices this virtually untapped dribbling style.

As soon as Broc can perform with ease the behind-the-back dribble, he shows it off to teammate Henry Maley who is non-plussed and walks away shrugging his shoulders. But fans are anything but indifferent.

As soon as Broc arrives in a gym, opposing fans begin booing.

Because of the behind-the-back dribble and various other ball-handling magic (common in today's play), Broc receives a lot of flak:

> Fans thought I was showing off; they'd boo and call me showboat among some of the nicer adjectives. I loved it. The opposing stu-

> dent body was always trying to upset me. The more they did it, the more I liked it.

Broc's mother, however, becomes so upset at one game she strikes another fan with her purse for making a disparaging remark about her son. What a mom!

3

VARSITY BUT GIRL HAPPY

Next season, however, as sophomores, Bud and Broc are reunited on the varsity playing for newly appointed head coach Arad McCutchan (former head coach Harry King had been inducted into the Navy). For the next three years, Bud and Broc play varsity ball together for the Bosse Bulldogs.

And playing for McCutchan who is innovative and progressive is very rewarding and satisfying. Bud credits him with teaching him to fake and roll much like Larry Bird. Grandpa too realizes Bud's potential quite early. His height, intelligence, and willingness to learn are tell-tale signs of greatness. With time and hard work, Bud becomes floor wise and quite a threat. He and Broc actively study the game and practice behind-the-back and blind passes relentlessly. In addition, Bud often gets the step on the defense.

Indeed, much of Bud's success comes from his prowess at getting position for the rebound and for his hook shot which he banks high off the backboard. For the jump ball, Bud boasts he pushes the opposing center with his left hand and tips the ball with his right. Since one official tosses the ball and the other checks the circle for trespassers, it's easy. He is not a great leaper, but he is 6-3.

And when shooting Bud banks almost all his shots because the basket is "larger" under the ball coming off the board than it is coming in clean, Bud affirms.

With World War II topping most headlines, War news, not basketball, is uppermost in every high school boy's mind. Upon graduation each boy faces compulsory military service. Few are deferred; fewer contest or object. Many boys adopt a *carpe diem* approach to high school: live for today, grasp the hour. And the team is no exception; they sow wild oats; they're out late, out of condition, and uncommitted.

Particularly adept at the practice of carousing are Bud and Broc who chase skirts and cavort almost nightly. When not chasing, for example, Broc is pursued by vivacious blonde heartthrob, Carolyn Kasler. Broc asserts their relationship was on again, off again. But, he adds, "I was very much enthralled by her and her beauty." A 5-3 slight, angelic-looking lass, Carolyn is said to sigh when

Broc passes (as many girls do). Broc likes her so much (he's *enthralled*) that she is one of *two* girls he takes to the Graduation Commencement Dance in 1945.

But, when Broc isn't with Carolyn, June Whetmer, dark, brunette Venus, also immensely enjoys his company. What a guy!

Finding a place to take a date isn't a problem for the players. Since school dances are extremely rare, dating usually consists of cruising Main Street, chatting car to car at the Humpty-Dumpty Drive-In Restaurant, and eating ice cream at Hermann's Ice Cream Shop. Getting a Coke and parking with your sweetheart is quite popular. Often the boys just skip the Coke. It's the War!

As a result, the team has little time to contemplate roundball, let alone practice or play it. Season record is poor. But the post-season tournament possesses an allure for the Bulldogs and offers a means to salvage a poor season.

Sanctioned by the Indiana High School Athletic Association (IHSAA), the state basketball tournament pits every participating prep school against every other despite enrollment, schedule, or record. Played at four levels—Sectional, Regional, Semi-Final and Final—it is the culmination of regular season play where *any* team can beat any *other* team *any* time.

So, when Hoosier Hysteria strikes home (officially dubbed the IHSAA Evansville Sectional),

A thing of beauty, Carolyn Kasler—Broc's girl

every Bosse player acquires immediate conviction to and new-found vigor for winning. At an unofficial team gathering, each pledges to compete with skilled abandon and to promote unanimity on the squad. To demonstrate their commitment, all sport crewcuts. Instantly basketball becomes their number one priority.

However, it's too little, too late! Despite the eleventh hour rally, Bosse's Bulldogs are edged out one point by Evansville Central in the opening game. Post game locker room emotion is feverish. Regret sits on faces like mud and tears fall like shower water. Broc learns yet another formidable lesson; when he witnesses the anguish, he vows never again as a Bulldog to endure it. When it counts, Broc pledges Bosse will ultimately triumph. Destiny.

Meanwhile, as varsity-reserve coach in 1943, Herman Keller discovers junior Gene Schmidt playing roundball in his physical education class—not on the team. Coach Keller immediately senses his talent and natural ability and inquires why he isn't playing on the team.

"I was cut, Mr. Keller," Schmidt explains. It seems former varsity coach Harry King ruled that by the time a boy is a junior he either plays varsity or doesn't play. Though perhaps a common rule, in this case it is a mistake.

Varsity Coach Arad McCutchan believes the rule to be without foundation and grants Coach

Keller permission to draft Schmidt onto the varsity-reserve. Destiny.

"Forever grateful" is the expression Schmidt uses to convey his appreciation to Coach Keller. "He became a father-figure to me," Schmidt explains. "He taught me almost everything I know about basketball."

Performing quite capably, he is the only Bulldog to play every reserve *and* varsity game without illness or injury.

Although Coach Keller doesn't discover any more of the "formidable five," he does learn Matthews runs flat-footed. Despite efforts at thwarting this plop-plop style, Matthews forgets. To prevent any recurrence, in practice Coach Keller often yells "Hey, Duck Foot!" Soon the sensitive, embarrassed Matthews no longer runs flat-footed. And, after a "cooling off period," he and Coach Keller even joke about it.

PART II

Broc, the littlest champion!

4

NEW COACHES, NICKNAMES, TALENTS, AND TALLIES

When the 1943-44 basketball season erupts, the Bulldogs are conditioned, electrified, and serious. Consisting of Norris Caudell, Gene Schmidt, and Bud, the front line average 6-3. Guard Jack Matthews is seventy-one inches tall, Broc only sixty-seven inches. During regular season Bud and Broc lead the team and the scoring. Despite grave efforts the squad posts only a marginal 9-7 record. Never at full strength, each week of the season a Bulldog is stricken with fever, flu, a cold, an injury. Ironically then no one realizes the team's capacity, its destiny—not even the players themselves.

While the rest of Evansville contributes to the War Effort by riveting fuselages for P-47 Aircraft, assembling LST's, reconditioning tanks, and manufacturing forty-five caliber machine-gun ammunition, at Bosse High School destiny is building a basketball dynasty in Norris Caudell, Gene Schmidt, Jack Matthews, Bud Ritter, and Broc Jerrel.

Like Harry King, varsity coach Arad McCutchan is inducted into the Navy. Taking over is varsity-reserve coach Herman Keller. Destiny.

Having come from coaching at Boonville High School where, he admits, he was fired, Keller is a lanky, rather tall Oakland City, Indiana native of German heritage. A man of few utterances, he never ridicules or yells at his charges. His philosophy of basketball is simple. He says he was told long ago that the best play in basketball is to get the ball through the hoop; the Bulldogs do it well. Courtside, he reveals his displeasure with grimaces and a profound display of foot stomping which becomes his trademark. More often, however, he is solemn and wise-looking. Aptly he is dubbed "The Abe Lincoln of Indiana High School Basketball."

As assistant to Varsity Coach Keller, Arvil Kilpatrick is praised by many as the embodiment of the perfect "number two" man. He is loyal, supportive, happy to play second fiddle to Coach Keller. To the team he is a booster, a coaxer, an intermediary for the Bulldogs. He designs the offense which consists of crisp ball handling—passing, working for easy, sure shots. And who initiates this type of floor play? The guards, namely Broc.

"The Abe Lincoln of
Indiana High School Basketball," Herman Keller

Giving the pep talk, Coach Kilpatrick can often still be heard cheering the team on and giving instructions as they leave the locker room. But, he does one thing that is quite unique in locker room gatherings. When Coach Keller explains a play, Coach Kilpatrick asks if the boys understand. To prove they do, he requires they actually run through the play in the locker room. What a coach!

For nicknames for the coaches, Matthews in his school newspaper column "On the Hardwood" dubs them "the *K* men."

Nicknames for the rest of the Bulldogs, however, are not so biting as Matthews' "Duck Foot." Early on, various and unusual tags surface; and among the starting five, they're rather conventional: Norris Caudell becomes "Norrie"; Gene Schmidt slides into "Smittie"; Julius Ritter is inexplicably "Bud"; Jack Matthews flows easily into "Mattie" (after Coach Keller buries "Duck Foot"). Of the starters, Broc's is the only really unconventional.

But, the second five take the trophy for nicknames.

Because Don Y. Tilley won't divulge the meaning of his middle initial, Broc dubs him "Yonicker"; otherwise, he's known as "Gravy Train" because he is brought up to varsity just before Sectionals. From their names, Gene Whitehead is called "Whitey" and Norm McCool "Mac." Often scoring only one point per game, Bill Hollman is called "One Point" Hollman.

MEET

THE

BOSSE

BULLDOGS!

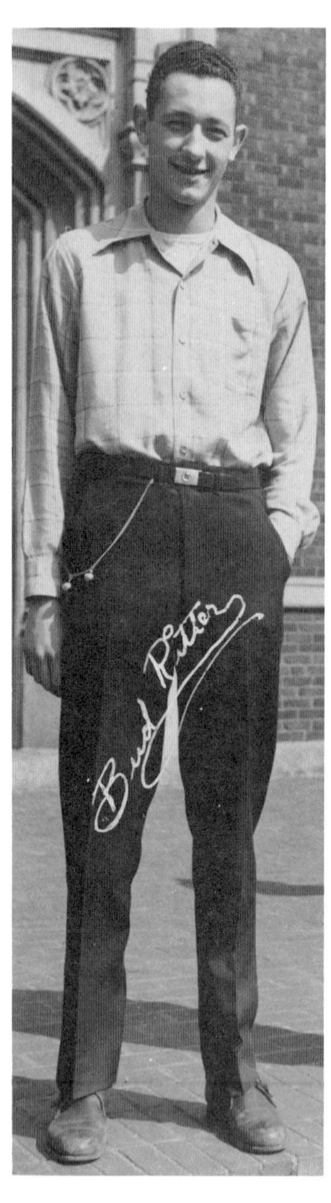

BUD RITTER
Age 16
Hgt. 6-3, Wgt. 180

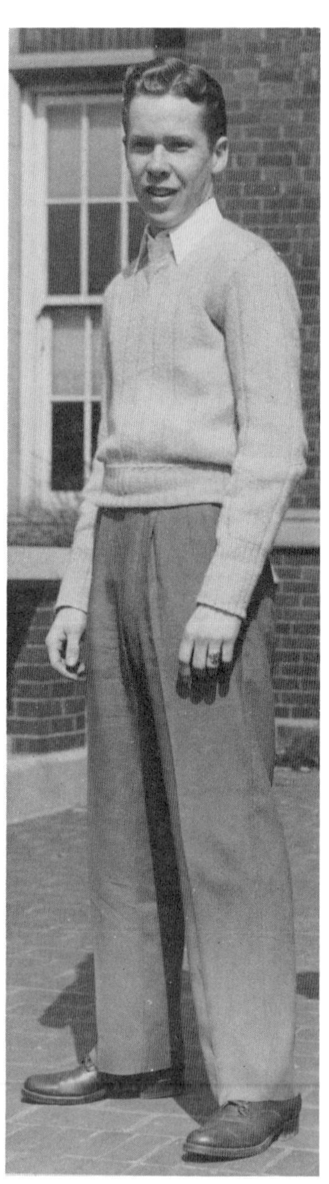

BROC JERREL
Age 17
Hgt. 5-7, Wgt. 130

NORRIS CAUDELL
Age 16
Hgt. 6-2, Wgt. 167

JACK MATTHEWS
Age 16
Hgt. 5-11, Wgt. 160

GENE SCHMIDT
Age 17
Hgt. 6-2, Wgt. 160

NORMAN McCOOL
Age 16
Hgt. 5-10, Wgt. 150

GENE WHITEHEAD
Age 16
Hgt. 5-11, Wgt. 165

DON TILLEY
Age 16
Hgt. 5-10, Wgt. 135

BILL HOLLMAN
Age 17
Hgt. 6-2, Wgt. 180

ERWIN SCHOLZ
Age 17
Hgt. 5-7, Wgt. 130

Finally for reasons unknown, Erwin Scholz answers to "Podjo" (like Bud and Broc, he still answers to his nickname).

Back to the "hardwood"! Broc is always trying to improve his shooting, his marksmanship. Off the court, he is a money player; he's a crack Twenty-one shooter and he proves it.

An excellent marksman, Broc spots almost anyone eighteen, takes the first shot, and always wins in Twenty-one. One of his easiest but most stubborn marks is Bulldog Ewing, former Washington Elementary School teammate; he just won't stop challenging Broc.

In game warfare, however, Broc typically fires from the area between the ten-second line and about one yard beyond the foul circle—sinking several is not unusual. Jumping as he shoots the two-hander, he is able to put his whole body harmoniously into it.

One of the hardest shots in basketball, the two-handed set must be released with the same strength from each hand. But, because one hand is usually stronger than the other, the shot is particularly difficult to execute. For this reason, shooting percentages are lower than todays. But, Broc still shoots the eyes out of 'em. There is much more to Broc than just long shooting, however.

Sports writer Cliff Guilliams states: "Besides being a brilliant ball handler and deadly outside shooter, Jerrel's other forte was his gift as a passer."

Broc explains it best! "They didn't really need to keep me from scoring but from throwing it to someone for a lay in." Since statistics for assists are not kept in 1944, there is no record of how many Broc had. But, they were many.

In 1944, the game is played somewhat differently than it is today. There is much ball control at which Broc is a magician, and game scores are lower. Here are a few rule changes.

A. Timeouts are of special note. Teams meet in their respective free throw circles. Not allowed to consult with the coach, the Bulldogs, under the leadership of Bud and Broc, must design, alter, rework offense and defense out on the floor to meet immediate needs.

Forthwith, during timeouts student manager "Fibber" McGeehee races onto the floor pushing a wagon containing towels and water to cool off the Bulldogs. Rather unique (only a couple exist in Indiana), the wagon has an image of a Bulldog's head painted on both ends and "Bosse" on each side. It is now on display in the Indiana Basketball Hall of Fame in New Castle, Indiana.

After deciding on strategy and toweling off, the Bulldogs spend extra time eyeing and pointing out good-looking girls in the bleachers. Bud and Broc are especially adept.

B. When fouled, the team may opt either to shoot a free throw or take the ball out. If behind, a team might prefer to take control of the ball.

Allowed only four fouls instead of five, players don't have the liberty of being too aggressive. In fact, in some important tournament games, both Bud and Matthews foul out.

Early March when Sectional tournament time arrives, no sane soul conceives Bosse's Bulldogs a threat after a 9-7 regular season.

But the team is already trying to get a winning edge with good luck charms and seemingly responsible behavior. For example, Gene Schmidt wears a thin coin in his right shoe. Bud is always the last man to run onto the floor. The starting five must always make their last shot in warm-up. Matthews *always* wears his fan-reknowned loud boxer shorts. And he wears number eight out of great reverence for Memorial High School football and basketball genius, Billy Hillenbrand. Even Matthew's father makes his contribution to team superstition by parking in the same spot at every game at Central Gym.

But, superstition cannot a winning team make.

Among Bulldog starters, each has a talent, a gift which enables him to achieve beyond the ordinary. Thus, the team is a cut above the competition. Schmidt has the uncanny sense of being in the most optimum spot to intercept a pass or pull down a rebound. Often assigned the most difficult opponent to guard, Matthews is a rabid defensive player. A string bean, Caudell is an extraordinary leaper.

In and out of the pivot as team center, Bud has no equal, hooking, passing, faking. In several games, in fact, he puts the ball between his legs, throws his arms into the air (completely faking his opponent), turns, puts up the leather for two.

Last and smallest, Broc does it all. Schmidt explains:

> He was light years ahead of the rest of us with his ability and light years ahead of his time. Broc could always produce when the game was on the line.

Ironically, however, Broc can't jump much higher than the paint on the free throw line.

And among the second five there is much talent too. Norm McCool is such an outstanding all-around athlete—especially excelling in baseball—that after college he is extended a major league baseball contract. Playing sixth man for the Bulldogs, he proves to be a very valuable substitute when Caudell or Schmidt foul out.

Podjo Scholz, too, is always ready to come in if needed. Although he "warms" the bench a majority of the time and frequently "debates" calls with officials, his enthusiasm, loyalty, and downright defense of every Bulldog strategy contribute immeasureably to team spirit and unity.

A scrapper with good speed, Yonicker Tilley shoots a tricky left-handed shot.

An aggressive player also, Gene Whitehead is a fine all-around athlete and ballplayer.

Finally, One Point Hollman is mystically true to his nickname, often scoring one free throw per game.

Destiny runs alongside these Bulldogs.

5

SEASON STREAKS, SKIDS, SHINES

To start the 1943-44 cage season, Bosse outstrips teams from three neighboring towns—Mt. Vernon, Winslow, and Ft. Branch. On a roll at 3-0, the Bosse Bulldogs next battle their first city opponent, West Side rival, Reitz Panthers.

West meets East in Central Gym where all city games are played. Uninjured and healthy, the Bulldogs are on the prowl.

Beginning sluggishly, the Reitz five score only four points first quarter against a strong Bosse start. Bosse 11-4—a very significant seven point edge, it proves.

Second segment, Reitz improves its defensive play slightly, whittling the lead to six, 22-16.

Despite a third period surge by flashy guard Groben, Reitz falls further back, 33-26.

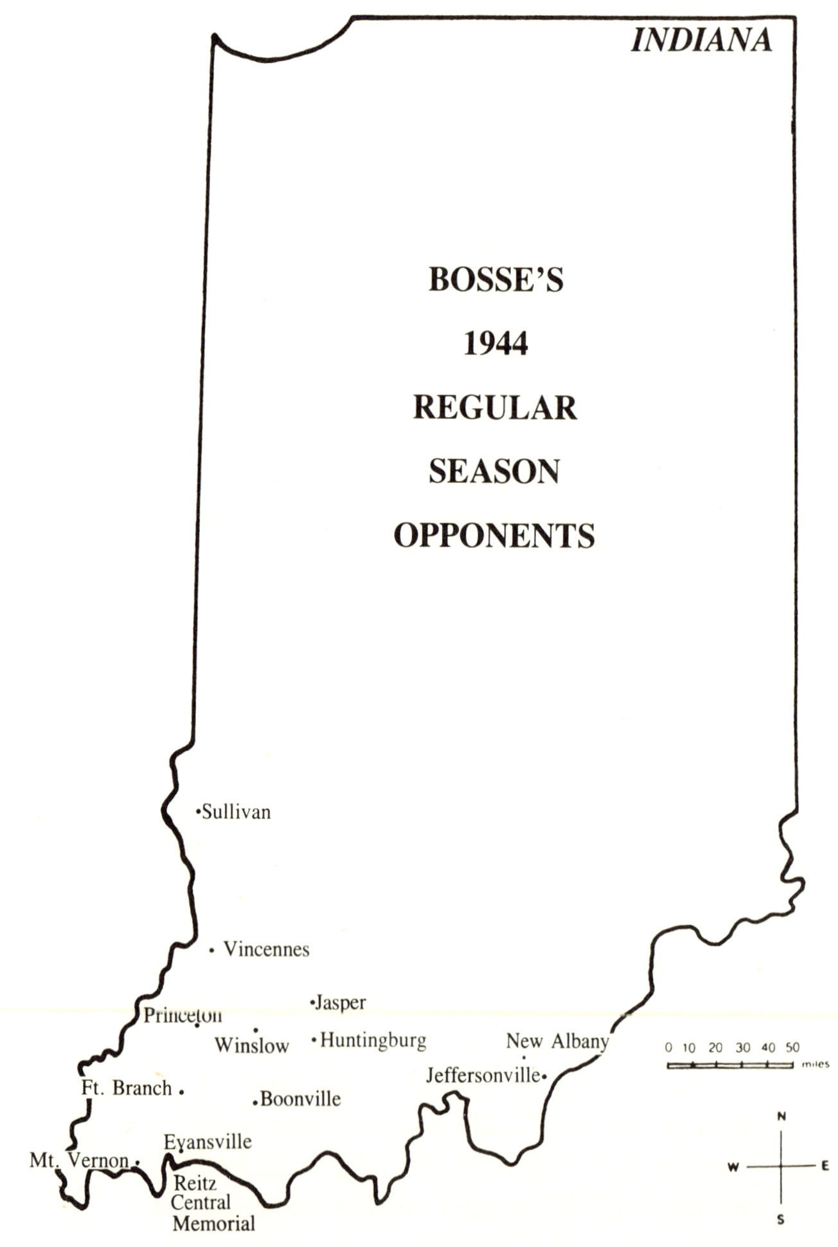
INDIANA
BOSSE'S
1944
REGULAR
SEASON
OPPONENTS
•Sullivan
• Vincennes
•Jasper
Princeton
Winslow
•Huntingburg
New Albany
Jeffersonville•
Ft. Branch •
•Boonville
Evansville
Mt. Vernon
Reitz
Central
Memorial
0 10 20 30 40 50
miles
N
W
E
S

Making a final drive fourth quarter, Reitz slinks up on the Bulldogs; and with only a few seconds it's Bosse 38-36. After Schmidt is whistled for a foul, Reitz chooses to take the ball out-of-bounds. In an uproar, fans clamor and stomp as time dwindles. But time doesn't save the Bulldogs; Bud does by intercepting a Reitz pass.

Bosse 38-36 over a stubborn, never-say-die Reitz five.

After winning the first four of its sixteen game season, Bosse tangles with neighborhood rival Memorial Tigers—alma mater of baseball great, Don Mattingly—no farther than nine or ten blocks from the Bulldogs on Evansville's Eastside.

Nearby neighbors, the two teams fight each battle of the athletic war tooth and nail. And the season's first cage battle between them justifies the rivalry. Neither team has the home court advantage, however, because all games are played in Central High School's Gym (Central Gym) whose capacity is 4200.

Although Broc scores a game high fifteen and dominates play swiping the ball and passing with precision, five minutes into third quarter Bud fouls out; play deteriorates; Bosse struggles. Broc's mid-court desperation shot to tie after a jump ball finds only dull metal. Final 27-25 Memorial.

Just blocks from Memorial High School, Grandpa and the Bulldogs meet after almost every game (as they do this night) in the kitchen of Bud's new home at 437 Rotherwood to discuss the game, scores, effective strategy, and future tactics. Into wee hours, they replay the games. But, on this particular evening, everyone searches for the elusive victory over the Memorial Tigers. It will come, but it will take time.

Next, the Bulldogs take on downtown foe Central Bears on their home floor—theirs is the only home court advantage. The Bulldogs are besieged by sickness, however; Bud is flu-stricken for weeks and doesn't even dress out; a victim of three-day measles, Broc dresses but doesn't reach the hardwood till midway through third period despite game-long pleas to Coach Keller.

The clash of these two powerhouses is often filled with thrills and mayhem. This encounter is no exception. In his *Evansville Press* column, Dick Anderson describes the scene: "Basketball hysteria dripped from the rafters in Central Gym last night. . . ."

First quarter action leads to an even, balanced game at seven all. In the second, however, Bosse falters, allowing Central a five-point advantage 15-10. As the third period opens, Central continues its mastery. Halfway through the period, Central leads 23-14—but here comes Broc. With Broc's entry Bosse perks, squeezing the gap at quarter's end to 24-22 Central.

Starting the fourth, McKinnis makes his foul shot compliments of Caudell. Central 25-22. Then Broc dribbles in and passes to Schmidt who drops it in. After a foul by Martin, Schmidt knots the score at 25. A thorn in the Bulldogs' side all evening, Central's Bawell cans one of his one-hand push shots. To counter, Broc races down the floor and lofts a one-hander which rips the nets.

Within seconds Schmidt taps in a missed shot; Broc follows with a twenty footer from the top of the circle. Hitting the back of the rim and bouncing high, it falls dead center. Bosse 31-27. The Dogs scent victory.

Central should buckle, but. . . on Broc's foul McKinnis drops in both tosses; Martin flashes under to tie at 31; Bawell heaves one to inch ahead 33-31. Bosse seems beaten, but McCool fights his way under to tie at 33. Although this is McCool's first varsity stint, he performs commendably. Overtime.

Opening the three-minute period, Matthews hits from far out, but Martin erases it with two. On Manis' foul Schmidt drops in a charity toss. Bosse 36-35. Now Broc stalls with clever dribbling, passing, maneuvering; but Gulledge crowds him and fouls out. After the out-of-bounds, Bawell too overplays Broc and fouls out.

Broc opts for the out-of-bounds (instead of the free throw). Why not? They're ahead one. But this time the Bulldogs err by not loosing a player for the pass. Time knifes the effort. Central's ball out.

After a few crisp passes, Martin wings in with about five seconds to play and scores. With four seconds, Broc calls time; but the Bulldogs can't get the ball down the hardwood before the gun.

A handsome Bulldog team takes a pause from practice.
Kneeling left to right: Broc Jerrel, Don Tilley, Norm McCool, Jack Matthews, Podjo Scholz
Standing left to right: Herman Keller, Norris Caudell, Bud Ritter, Bill Hollman, Gene Schmidt, Gene Whitehead, Arvil Kilpatrick

In bedlam, the gym shudders; Central coach Glen Bretz stands yelling "The game is over!" Hoisting Martin to their shoulders, his teammates carry him triumphantly to their dressing room. Yet, the Bulldogs follow dejected. Central 37-36. Destiny.

What have the Bulldogs learned from this loss? Perhaps it is to shoot the free throw (score points) and not take the ball out-of-bounds. Hindsight.

Bosse scrambles, falters, surges, loses. Score points for valor and pluck but none for victory. Bosse must regroup *and* recover.

With Bud again on the sick list, the Bulldogs suffer their third straight defeat at the hands of a tough crew from visiting Huntingburg High School. At Central Gym the squad from the small town of Huntingburg peeps by the Bosse Bulldogs 36-35. Season 4-3.

Located across the Ohio River from Louisville in Southeastern Indiana—some 90 winding miles away—the Jeffersonville High School Red Devils represent an even more formidable foe. Though a prized friend of Coach Keller's, Jeffersonville Coach Ed Lyskowinski would probably prefer beating the Bulldogs to gorging himself with a bountiful meal after a fast.

Into Central Gym the Red Devils bring a respectable 9-2 record.

Starting with a rush, the Bulldogs stack up an 11-6 lead though playing almost the entire quarter without Bud. Near quarter's end, he enters, sparking the Bullodgs even further. With Bud banging the boards, Jeffersonville never threatens and the Bulldogs close the half ahead 23-17.

For the third, both teams employ fire department tactics (Jeffersonville in particular), frequently heaving the leather the length of the hardwood and fast-breaking. Despite the withering pace, the Bulldogs hold up, often benefiting from the "two on one" play. At the stop it's Bosse 37-27.

The fourth finds both teams swapping baskets with Bosse never crowded. Bud, Caudell, and Schmidt lead scoring with 13, 12, and 9 respectively. Having left his "shooting eye" at home, states reporter Dick Anderson, Broc dazzles the Red Devils with expert dribbling, confident floor work, *and* crisp feeds to Bud, Caudell, and Schmidt—the fruits of which were just cited. Bosse smacks Jeffersonville 48-39.

Among spectators is Jasper High School Coach Leo "Cabby" O'Neill, scouting for his Wildcats who will challenge the Bulldogs in a couple of weeks in Central Gym. Of Bosse he predicts: "Now, brother, you are talking about a ball club that is going to cause a lot of people headaches!" Destiny?

Ncxt day, the Bulldogs motor about seventy miles north of Evansville to blunt the Sullivan Golden Arrows 36-19. After opening a 14-4 first period lead, the Bulldogs never look back. With 11, Bud is high point man. All seems well; the Bulldogs are again on a roll. All are well.

Destiny?

6

FLOOR TACTICS AND MORE

Throughout the season the Bulldogs use a number of different, sometimes deceptive, usually creative, often successful game tactics in order to win. One of them involves free throws.

The best free-throw shooter on the team, Broc shoots underhanded as do other team members.

Second-best shooter is Bud. As second-best, however, often he doesn't shoot his own free throws. Instead of stepping to the charity stripe, Bud prepares to snare the rebound—should *Broc* miss. That's right! Broc! Since Broc is the best, he shoots the free throw. Here's how!

While one referee calls out numbers, the other lines up players for the rebound. Because one *offensive* man is allowed first position for the rebound, Bud takes post position on the right side for the rebound; Broc shoots. To the anger of countless opponents, Bud and Broc succeed in this deception fifteen or twenty times during the season. But that's not all!

If the team needs one point, Broc sinks the toss. But if the team needs two, Broc can make the ball strike the left arc of the hoop, bounce up and off the backboard, and down into the waiting hands of Bud who puts it back for two. After much practice they can do it almost every time they want. Hoop work.

Another popular play is the out-of-bounds, frequently used by the Bulldogs. It consists of Matthews taking the ball out under the Bulldogs' basket. Although Matthews intends to pass in to Caudell, Caudell shouts to Matthews in great acting style, "Hey, I'm supposed to take it out on this play!" The defense relaxes. At that point, Matthews flip-passes the ball to Caudell for an exceptionally easy deuce. Almost always good for two when two are needed. Pass work.

When the team travels, Coach Keller usually drives Norm McCool, Bud Ritter, Jack Matthews, and Broc in his car. Keller especially likes to talk to the boys in the back seat and often simply looks back at them as he speaks; the boys are usually anxious and edgy about it and feel especially uncertain as they travel the 100 miles east to New Albany—the two lane road is hilly, curvy, and narrow. However, the team arrive intact for the season's tenth clash against the New Albany Bulldogs.

Once there, however, no hotel accommodations have been made for the team (conserving for the War Effort?); and they spend many of the pre-game hours in a very hot locker room on narrow, uncomfortable benches trying to relax, sleep, somehow pass the time.

During that long wait, the usual Bulldog locker room looks and sounds like this: Schmidt is tucking that thin lucky coin into his shoe; Matthews is tugging on his colorful but outragious boxer shorts; Caudell is rehearsing his lines and blocking for the tricky in-bounds play between him and Matthews.

To ease tensions, players are bouncing balls off walls all around the room. Pulling on his protective leather and felt knee pads, Broc is delivering one-liners to Yonicker and Podjo. Players, managers, trainers are everywhere encouraging each other in the upcoming bout. Meanwhile, Bud waits for everyone to exit the locker room so he can be the last man onto the hardwood.

The New Albany game is hard fought and one incident deserves mention.

In the third quarter, Broc is involved in a jump ball; however, as soon as he's called to jump he dashes out of the circle, and Matthews (the best jumper on the team?) saunters in to jump. Momentarily, officials suffer a memory lapse, allowing Matthews, not Broc, to jump. New Albany fans are all but frothing to no avail. Bosse gets the tip and the crucial possession.

After the game, Coach Herman Keller and New Albany Coach Charlie McConnell discuss major events of the contest. An even-tempered man, a paragon of character, a kind and good human being, Coach McConnell, however, blurts after the game, "Nice game, Herman. But, I'll be damned if I appreciate Jerrel trying to help referee the game!"

McConnell was never known to use curse words or other off-color language. This is not the first, nor is it the last time Broc "referees" a game. In scoring, Broc dazzles foe and friend with a game high thirteen.

Covering the game, the *Louisville Courier-Journal* prints: "Jerrel, ace dribbler and speed merchant. . . took the situation. . . ."

Another article touts Broc as "a half-pinter who handles a basketball as if it were about the size of a billiard ball." In spite of the "heat," Bosse by two, 29-27, over New Albany.

7

WIN, LOSE, KISS; COLD, FRACTURE, WHIMPER

Just thirty miles north of Evansville is the modest-sized county seat of Princeton, home of the Tigers. When they prowl around Central Gym, they give the Bulldogs a stiff fight in Bosse's eleventh game. Officiated by veterans, Ox Hartley and Bob Hudson, 31 fouls are whistled throughout the game—several on Broc in the first period; and, Schmidt fouls out right after the fourth begins.

In the first period, Princeton can only manage two field goals and three free throws. Bosse is hotter with five and two respectively. Despite the good scoring, Broc tallies three fouls and is replaced by Podjo. After eight minutes Bosse 12-7.

In the second Princeton surges, tying at 15. At half, it's Bosse 17-15.

Broc sparkles from start to finish second half, compensating for his poor start. The Bulldogs command a 26-20 lead to end third quarter play.

As the fourth begins, it seems to swing in favor of the Princeton Tigers. Schmidt fouls out here with Bosse up 26-25. The end looks bleak. But "in times of stress and peril in the last eight minutes," Jimmy Fraser reports, Broc scores three field goals and three charity tosses to thwart any Tiger push. Nabbing scoring honors, Broc pours in 14. Of Broc's shooting and ball handling clinic, Tom Stokes states in his newspaper column: "It called to mind the old cliche about 'you hold still and I'll dance around you!' " Final Bosse 37-30.

There is a bit of a fuss about the foot stomping and shrieking by Bosse fans as Princeton shoots free throws, but it probably didn't decide the game. Bosse's eighth victory.

Next, Bosse tangles with intrepid Jasper in the twelfth match-up.

Predominately comprised of German descendants, Jasper is about sixty-five miles northeast of Evansville among rolled hills and the simple stubble-brown beauty of nature in late autumn. Rivalry between the Jasper Wildcats and any Evansville school is less than beauteous; it is fierce. The competition is effectively fueled by formidable Jasper mentor Cabby O'Neill whose Wildcats always threaten as they do this evening.

At this juncture in the cage season, Broc leads Evansville city scoring with 107. On Jasper, Broc drops in another game high thirteen—fruitlessly, however. Before 3500 in Central Gym, Jasper prevails 36-32.

Crowning of Bosse basketball queen, Fern Barning, provides a pleasing interlude in an otherwise uneventful second clash with Bosse's West Side rival, Reitz Panthers. In the earlier season encounter, Bosse squeaked past 38-36. But the current meeting yields a decisive victory 46-25 with Bud's fifteen and Broc's twelve sufficient to declaw the Panthers in the Dogs' thirteenth outing.

The evening's most dramatic moment occurs center court at half as acting captain Broc ambles center circle and unabashedly kisses Miss Barning with all the charm and audacity of Clark Gable. Fans are delirious.

Next adversary is the Central Bears in Central Gym. Before 4000 rabid, often belligerent, fans in the dimly lighted arena, Bosse bows; but again the Bulldogs are not at full strength. Once more Bud must sidestep play because of a chest cold. Final Central 36-32.

Next game pits the Bulldogs against Keller's former coaching home, Boonville, twenty miles east of Evansville.

With season's end lurking, Bosse travels to Boonville for game fifteen in unexplainably cold Clarke Gym. Near zero temperatures outside shadow cold Bosse shooting inside.

Is that Clark Gable or Broc Jerrel?
Miss Barning, Bosse Basketball Homecoming Queen, knows for sure.

Such an inadequate barn-like facility, the gym still has gymnastics rings hanging over the playing floor. On one particularly lofty shot, Matthews' ball hits a ring and is whistled out of bounds.

Scoring just nine of sixty-nine, Bosse staggers. Some very sticky guarding of Broc by Dick Whitney limits Broc to only nine points. Although Coach Keller badly wants this win over his previous coaching home, Bosse is frozen out 38-27.

Further diminishing Bosse's potential and dashing hopes, Broc breaks the knuckle bone of the forefinger on his left hand in first quarter play against Boonville. The consequences could be tragic. Almost a quarter-inch of bone is broken away. At the same time, Bud is still ailing. Fears are both Bud and Broc will be side-lined for Sectionals only days hence.

But, the final season match at Vincennes is yet to be played.

When the Bullodgs bark at the Vincennes Alices 50 miles north in poorly lighted Adams Coliseum, their bite ironically is even less severe. With two top dogs limping badly—seeing only a brief part of the Vincennes' dog fight—the Bullpups whimper away defeated. Vincennes Alices by two, 30-28.

8

PRE-TOURNAMENT HYPE

The season is not championship caliber; at 9-7 there's not a whole lot to brag about. So what's next? The granddaddy of all Indiana basketball competition: The Indiana High School Athletic Association (IHSAA) Basketball tournament. March Madness! Hoosier Hysteria! In Evansville, as in several Indiana cities and towns, the first round play is the Sectional. To the victor goes the cherished game nets, prestigious trophies, plaques, rings, fame, and more.

But, the Bulldogs are staggering with two starters almost in the dog hospital. That's right! It's Hoosier Hysteria, though, and *anything* can happen.

Boosting the team, however, two Bulldogs receive significant accolades. Bud and Broc are voted onto the Southern Indiana Athletic Conference (SIAC) first team. Though not receiving the highest vote totals, Bud accumulates nineteen and Broc twenty-one. The distinction helps console Broc, but no doubt he's looking to Indianapolis' Butler Fieldhouse with State Championship hopes.

Just before the Sectional, however, yet another disappointment visits the Bulldogs. When the Associated Press publishes its Indiana High School Basketball Poll, Bosse is not even in the top ten. Anderson High School's intrepid Indians receive 164 votes, Bulldogs a meagre one. And remember during the regular season, the team lost seven games.

Perhaps it was because every time the "Beat 'Em, Bulldogs!" sign was taped to the front hall wall of Bosse High School the team lost. So just before Sectionals, the team requests the sign be removed from the front hall. It is. That's one point in the Bulldogs' favor.

Even "oddsmakers" bet against Bosse. Hanging around gym practices is ardent sports fan, Ralph McCool, Norm's brother. From him, Bud and Broc learn odds against Bosse's winning the Sectional are 3-1. Determined to prove the bookies wrong, Bud and Broc make a small wager the Bulldogs *will* win.

In boosting the Bulldogs, the student cheering section plays a significant role. Prior to Sectional play, Bosse principal Carl Eifler announces that any student with a Sectional ticket will be excused from school Thursday and Friday, February 24 and 25 to attend the games. Basketball fever.

All season, team members receive notes and letters of encouragement and adoration from fellow students, admirers, well-wishers. Attached to lockers, note-books, and placed in Jack Matthews' 1934 Chevrolet Convertible—nicknamed the Green Hornet—they are an inspiration to the team. Most of the messages and autograph requests, however, come to Broc who is urged to buy a rubber stamp to avoid writer's cramp.

Local barber "Red" Kroeger promises each Bulldog player and coach a free haircut, shampoo, facial, manicure, and pedicure if the Bulldogs win the State Championship. Popular with the team, Red is a major backer and avid sports enthusiast.

But, unrated and injured, the Bulldogs appear to pose no threat to anybody in post-season tournament play.

PART III

9

SECTIONAL: FROM MT. VERNON TO MEMORIAL

Opening its Sectional competition at Central Gym, Bosse defeats all-black Booker T. Washington High School of Mt. Vernon, Indiana. Despite that broken left index finger from the Boonville game, Broc plays as if in fittest shape. To facilitate the use of his injured left hand, the fractured index finger is taped to his middle digit which serves as a splint. Although Broc doesn't score, the Bulldogs glide past Mt. Vernon Washington a whopping 42 points. Final 62-20.

Plucking scoring honors are guard, Jack Matthews and forward, Gene Schmidt with 16 and 14 respectively. His basketball prowess beginning to peak (and what better time), Matthews hones his talents which come alive in shooting and on defense in this game. Bud's temperature stabilizes as his lung infection wanes; Broc continues playing with a four-digit left hand. Though impaired, the Bulldog pack rumbles on.

In the second Sectional game, Evansville's West Side meets East Side before 4200 as F. J. Reitz and Bosse claw it out. For the first ten minutes of play, neither team tallies a field goal; then Reitz christens the hoop on a field goal. For three and a half quarters, Reitz plays the Bulldogs evenly; however, behind Bud's game high 13 and phantom-like defense, Bosse spurts to a 32-25 victory.

After the game both Bosse coaches run onto the floor to shield Bud and Broc from rushing fans. They don't want their stars harmed. Now, Bud's fever is only on the playing floor. Despite Broc's broken index finger, he throws in nine as Bosse plods towards Sectional triumph.

Advancing to the Sectional Semi-Final, the Bulldogs tangle with the Evansville Lincoln Lions, an all-black East Side school. Explosive, the Lions have eliminated New Harmony High School in the highest game point total of the Evansville Sectional, 64-46. Bosse seems a sure winner; but, beginning the second quarter, Bud and Cal Martin collide midcourt hitting each other in their knees. As fans raise heavy moans and desperate prayers, Bud hobbles to the showers.

Strangely, Lincoln suffers more from Bud's absence as their offense slumps. At half, Bosse leads 22-16. Assigned the duty of guarding Lincoln's ace guard, Cal Martin, Matthews dogs him, constantly getting in front of him and waving his arms in his face. So rabid is Matthews, he is called for face-guarding and fouls out; but, not before he holds Martin to just 16.

Despite net-shredding attempts by Lincoln bomber Cal Martin (38 points against New Harmony), the Lions falter second half. With Bud back and Caudell leaping, the Dogs monopolize the boards; Schmidt fires in 11 in his best game in months. Capping the Bosse onslaught, Broc directs the movement of the leather with clever dribbling and awesome coolness. As Broc contributes 12, the Bulldogs digest the Lions 49-31.

Of concern, however, is Bud's ankle, more severely injured than first realized despite his Trojan effort in the Lincoln game. Still in much pain, he fears he will be of no help on the floor that night against leviathan Memorial. After the game he is taken to the Vendome Hotel to rest on specially set-up cots in a small meeting room. Hot water is poured over the swollen ankle. But, the ankle responds only slightly. Bud is somber and frustrated, anxious about the Memorial game. Destiny.

So badly injured, Bud almost faints en route on foot four blocks back to Central Gym for the championship bout with Memorial; the boys catch him as he falls against a building. To encourage him, Broc sidles up and asks him "How much do you want us to beat 'em by, Bud?" The boys, especially Broc, are that certain they can win.

A major factor in his ultimate recovery is a treatment known in veterinary stalls as a horse poultice. That afternoon, Ox Hartley, son of veterinarian Dr. Hartley, applied it to Bud's ankle. Here's what it is and does.

A powder mixed with warm water and scented with wintergreen, the poultice becomes jelly-like and is spread like cake icing about one-fourth inch thick on the ankle. Then, the ankle is covered with a cloth and wrapped with an ace bandage. In effect, it draws out swelling and pain. More than once it is used by the Bulldogs.

Next stop, final Sectional game against "archest" of rivals, the Memorial Tigers, whose den, you recall, is but blocks from Bosse's kennel.

Memorial played the 1:30 P.M. game Saturday, Bosse the 2:30 P.M. game. It's now evening; city Titans, Memorial and Bosse, are about to clash. And who won the regular season bout, you muse? 27-25 Memorial.

Telling him the team just needs his presence on the hardwood, Keller encourages Bud. So he almost hobbles end to end posturing himself under each basket. In spite of the ankle, miraculously Bud turns in a splendid performance hooking, rebounding, shooting. Here's how the match progresses.

It's 7:30 P.M., Central Gym, 4200 bipartisan, fanatic-like "spectators." The Evansville precinct of Hoosier Hysteria is fever-pitched.

Memorial snags the tip but can't put it in the hoop. After each team misses, Broc steals a pass and heaves the first long shot for two. From the charity stripe, Memorial gets its first several points. Finally, however, Vic Kissel rattles a long one through for Memorial. Matthews hits for Bosse and Broc thieves another, puts it up, misses, but follows for two. Hustle! With Bosse 7-4, Memorial motions time-out. With ease, Broc scores on one of two attempts underneath. At quarter's end Bosse 11, Memorial 6.

Monopolizing on several Memorial errors, the Bulldogs mount a 16-6 lead. Despite substitutions the Tigers are not sparked. Gene Logel cans a long shot, but Bud pops a one-hander from the foul circle. Between Matthews' and Broc's two pointers, Memorial's Reinhart posts a deuce. Amidst several free tosses for Memorial, Bosse closes the half well ahead 25-11.

Grabbing the tip-off again second half, Memorial's Kissel tries to play catch-up, but he misses his first toss. Icy Memorial can't get warm, scoring three to Broc's six. Although Bud limps, the Dogs vault; and despite Broc's splinted index finger, he dribbles fancy circles around the Tigers using the behind-the-back dribble to engineer unseen moves. As the period closes, Bosse is at the charity stripe tallying points; Memorial is still staggering, posting 19 to Bosse's 34.

Exchanging fouls, both teams play raggedy, hacking, shoving, chopping, pushing. About halfway through the final period, it's Bosse 41-25. With the entrance of subs Don Tilley, Podjo Scholz, and Gene Whitehead, the end is obvious. Except for the early minutes of the first quarter, Memorial has never been in the contest. Bosse 46, Memorial 29. Final!

Perhaps Memorial's frustration is best reflected in Coach Art "Rusty" Cosgrove's game-long chewing of a flat stick as he watches his talented team fall like Humpty Dumpty. And, when he leaves the gym, he hits the panic bar, slams the door open, and runs out angry and disappointed, saying very little to anyone.

So the Bulldogs prevail. The Bulldogs are now acclimated to Head Coach Herman Keller; Bud's swollen ankle responds to treatment. To promote the healing, Ox Hartley stops by Bud's home each day through the following Wednesday to apply the horse poultice; he starts a light workout with the team on Thursday (Regional begins Saturday). But Bud'll be ready! His fever too is subsiding; his lungs are clear.

However, Broc's broken index finger is only slowly healing.

Broc's performance against Memorial is splended. In Jimmy Fraser's column in *The Evansville Sunday Courier and Press,* there are nothing but plaudits for Broc. Fraser writes:

> Bosse High School's Bulldogs, led by the brilliant dribbling and shooting of the red-

> haired Bryan Jerrel, defeated Memorial. . . . The one hundred thirty pound bundle of basketball brilliance dazzled the crowd despite playing with a broken index finger. . . .

Local sports writer Dick Anderson declares Broc "turned in a dazzling exhibition [and] probably played his best game in a Bosse uniform." Does Broc deserve the accolade? Most assuredly! But, winning will take Broc *and* Bud, Schmidt, Caudell, Matthews, and all the subs playing as a unit; any player in a pick-up game knows that.

Evansville Sectional Champs for 1944—The Bosse Bulldogs.

10

REGIONAL: CAN AN ACE OR A PIONEER BEAT A BULLDOG?

The Regional looks like a cinch; Schmidt kisses his good luck coin. Matthews' horseshoe still lies in his school locker. And all the parents are dutifully parking in their favorite spots. Triumph is (must be) imminent!

In the Evansville Regional at Central Gym, the Boonville Pioneers tangle with the Princeton Tigers first at 1:30. An hour or so later, the Dale Aces meet the Bosse Bulldogs.

Boonville whips Princeton 33-24. And Bosse lashes Dale 38-27 but not before Bud *re*-injures that pesky ankle. Again Ox Hartley applies a wintergreen poultice to Bud's ankle to draw out the pain and reduce swelling.

The Boonville Pioneers are big, capable and tough to overcome as the Bulldogs learn. Despite resting all afternoon in the Vendome Hotel. Bud's condition is still tenuous. After a light dinner, the team begins the familiar four block trek to Central Gym on foot, but Bud rides. Weak and in great pain, he still has a quite swollen ankle.

It's 7:30 P.M. Central Gym where 4500 uproarious fans watch furious, helter-skelter basketball, terminating in flaring tempers and flailing limbs from Boonville and Bosse players alike.

On guts, Bud plays, aided largely by trainer/football coach Phil Bevarly's excellent ankle taping.

Although Boonville center, Alva Collins, is bigger and heavier and tries to push Bud around, Bud uses finesse, quickness, and experience to outplay him.

Commanding the tip, Boonville's Edney hits his left-hand specialty. High and spirited, the Pioneers instantly dominate play and at one point even steal the ball from Broc himself. But, behind Bud and Caudell, Bosse rallies. Broc hits a long one; Boonville counters. Quarter's end Boonville 9, Bosse 8.

Second quarter Boonville keeps pressure on. The lead see-saws, but Boonville's drive seems to bewilder the Dogs. Then, Bosse spurts on Schmidt's pass to Bud who scores and on Caudell's side shot which hits the mark. When Bosse edges ahead 16-13, the Pioneers manage to recover and tie at 17; then, they surge following a six point flurry by Edney. At half Boonville 23, Bosse 18.

The proverbial barn is burning out of control!

The Bulldogs need a boost and everyone wonders whence it will or can come. Dribbling to the corner, Matthews sifts through the defense, twists, and hits a one-hander. Bosse is charged; Broc follows suit. Now it's Boonville 23-22.

Again Matthews hits from the corner. Pioneers call time. Before quarter's end, Matthews connects on another from out; soon it's Bosse 28-26. Matthews cracks the often dead-locked game and provides the continuing flame of energy for the Bulldogs.

Boonville now is shaky as gym, fan, and player temperatures rise steadily. Scoring two, Boonville's Skelton uncovers a glimmer of Pioneer hope. But, for the first time, Bud comes out of the pivot to connect; Schmidt is fouled, enraging Boonville's Edney who is called for a *T* (technical) for abusive language (in a 1944 high school basketball game?).

Behind scores from Bud and Schmidt, the Bulldogs vault; Boonville is buried. But, shortly after getting two, Bud scrambles for a ball and falls, grabbing at his left leg. During time-out, he limps to the sidelines and is replaced by a sub.

Then, without warning, tempers pop; vying for the ball, Broc steps on Boonville's Anderson who's been guarding him roughly. Both are waved to the sidelines with Podjo (off the bench) after displaying signs of switching from basketball to boxing. And somewhere in the melee, a Pioneer accidentally scores two in the Bosse basket. As second stringers take over, Boonville's hopes are dashed; their drive goes pfftt. Bosse wins its fifth Evansville Regional 43-35.

Coach Keller now begins conducting closed practices in the Bosse Gym. With the exception of Dr. Harry Whetstone, a very loyal Bosse supporter, and Grandpa, the general public is no longer allowed to watch the Bulldogs and learn their strategy. Wisdom.

11

SEMI-FINAL: PART I—MENTAL QUIRK, MOORESVILLE, MASSAGE

The tallest team in the "Sweet Sixteen"[1] at five feet eleven inches, the Bulldogs now look to combat at Vincennes Coliseum in the Semi-Final against the Mooresville Pioneers. In his column "On the Hardwood" in the Bosse *School Spirit* newspaper, Matthews assures his readers with "Again I say we'll do everything in our power to come through for dear ol' Bosse.

. . . WE CAN, WE MUST AND WE WILL."

First, however, the Washington Hatchets must chop through Bedford's Stonecutters in the 1:30 P.M. opener.

At 9:00 A.M. about 1000 Evansville Bosse boosters drive their private cars to the site of

[1]There are four Semi-Final sites around the state with four teams in each.

Vincennes' Semi-Final 50 miles north. To make the drive, Bosse backers have saved gas rationing stamps for weeks and paid $1.50 for one of the 5454 seats in Vincennes' John Adams Coliseum.

In the first game, the Washington Hatchets test the Bedford Stonecutters. After a sluggish start (scoreless for six minutes), the Hatchets carve a measly 8 to 6 half-time edge. Second half, Washington keeps cooler, surviving through clever stalling. In the defensive battle—score is knotted eight times—the Hatchets avenge their two losses to Bedford by outlasting the Stonecutters 20-16. Washington will be the entertainer for the winner of the Mooresville—Bosse face-off.

The Washington Hatchets exit the floor delirious and jubilant enroute to their dressing room adjacent to Bosse's. Bosse waits to play the second afternoon game. Entrance to the Hatchets' locker room, however, is accessible only by passing right through Bosse's locker room. As the Washington team races by hooting, cheering, boasting about going to State (they had won back to back in '41 and '42), they assure each other victory is already in the bag in the evening game. The Bulldogs sit, mouths agape with eyes like moons. The incident provides a keen example of what Coach Keller terms a "mental quirk," an advantage to any team. More about that shortly.

When the Bulldogs leap ahead 14 to 5 against Mooresville, a rout appears imminent to the sellout crowd of 5454. But Mooresville's Pioneers surge back to lead 25-24 early in the third quarter.

Bosse fans are chilled. To the rescue races Broc, the little red-head, dribbling down the floor to fire a long one; the Bulldogs will not look back.

At the beginning of the fourth, the Dogs sit up with a 32-29 advantage. Bud hits from inside; Schmidt adds two under, and McCool makes a three-point play on a lay-up. Now it's 41-31. At the gun it's 46-33. Dan Scism writes in *The Evansville Courier:*

> Jerrel's floor work stood out and his clever dribbling amused the fans, some of whom wouldn't have bet he couldn't dribble a field goal through.

After the Mooresville victory, the Bulldogs relax in the Lincoln Hotel where they stay two in a room. Giving rub downs is ardent team backer and positive force, "Cheerio" Carrico.

Cheerio is a big, jolly Bosse alumnus who follows the team everywhere. Busy giving the starting five rub-downs with cocoa butter, he doesn't have time for the second five. Since Yonicker (Tilley) is on the second five, he gives *himself* a rub-down, saying he needs it because he might get in the Washington game. Although the massage keeps Podjo awake, he doesn't complain so Yonicker continues massaging.

No doubt the Bulldogs are bold. In the return walk from the Lincoln Hotel to the Vincennes Coliseum for the championship game, Bud asks Dr. Whetstone to keep his pocket knife till after the game because he wants to use it to cut down the nets after they win. Confidence! Destiny?

Next victim? Washington's Hatchets in the final game of the Vincennes Semi-Final at 8:00 P.M.

Coach Keller readily admits he's no Vince Lombardi of locker room speakers; but before the Bulldogs meet the Hatchets, he musters a message. Before the game he tells his charges there is probably no need to play since Washington is already convinced it will win; they even told the Bulldogs so as they clamored through the Bosse dressing room earlier that day.

Well, that is the critical factor, the "mental quirk," separating the teams. The Dogs now go out to play with fire in their eyes and victory on their minds.

12

SEMI-FINAL: PART II—FROM BRILLIANCE TO A BONFIRE

Before 5050 fans, the favorite Washington Hatchets battle the Bulldogs start to finish. Washington star Frank Gilkinson and Broc go head to head the entire 32 minutes. First quarter stop, it's Washington 8, Broc 8. Indeed at one point in the game, Gilkinson races down the hardwood, shaking his head as if to say, "I can't guard that little red head!"

Ahead at half 20-17, the Dogs nose victory. But, Washington puffs into a 21-20 lead. After the lead see-saws, the third buzzer finds Bosse ahead 29-27.

With three minutes remaining, Broc sinks one from near the ten second line to put the Bulldogs ahead three, 32-29. Now Bosse stalls to protect a fragile edge.

In the final two minutes of the fourth, the Hatchets bag a free throw. Fans stand erect as Washington's McCracken ties, but Broc counters. At this point each time Broc brings the leather down court, Washington Hatchet fans jeer and hiss; and each time he shoots they wail, "Ohhh!" When Washington's Allison powers through for a tip-in, Broc reciprocates with two from the side.

After the Bulldogs tally a free throw, they lead 37-34. Again Bosse stalls.

As Broc controls the leather, with Johnny Wooden's touch, Washington's Allison sprawls on the hardwood, pawing at the basketball which Broc dribbles just out of his reach. One minute remains.

While Broc is surrounded by three or four menacing Hatchets, trying to swipe the ball, he spots Bud alone underneath and rolls the ball to him between the defenders' legs. "It was the only way I could get the ball to him!" Broc explains. Bud widens the gap to five.

With just seconds, Gilkinson fouls Bud who bags the final point. But not without some drama. As Bud prepares to shoot the free throw, Washington fans again jeer and boo. Like a businessman, Broc struts to the Washington cheering section. Waving his arms to signal "No" in teacher-like style, he is unable to quell them. Although Hatchet fans scowl at him and shout even louder, Broc is having the time of his life. Washington 34, Bosse 40. The Hatchets are dulled.

Jimmy Fraser reports in *The Evansville Sunday Courier and Press:* "Jerrel came through with an amazing performance . . . . The little red-head. . . bewildered the Hatchets with his dazzling dribbling and all-around floor work." Fraser states he could spend fifteen minutes searching the dictionary for adjectives to describe Broc's play and the Bosse Bulldogs' performance.

He concludes his column with this assertion:

> If Broc was brilliant in taming Memorial's Tigers in the Sectional Final, he was magnificent this evening in making the Hatchets squirm in anguish.

Scoring 9 field goals, a Semi-Final record (many from near the ten-second line), and four charity tosses, Broc leads scorers with 22, handles the ball smoothly, moves with cunning. Overall, he sparks teammates to victory. Indeed, after two minutes of watching Broc and the Bulldogs, legendary coach John Adams knows Bosse will triumph. And, with that soft, caressing touch on the ball, Broc plays his finest game to date.

His counterpart, Washington's Frank Gilkinson, is responsible for keeping the Hatchets in competition with key plays, difficult dribbling feats, and keen passing. He scores 7 goals and one free throw for 15. Fine effort in most any game—for naught against dreadnaught Bosse.

In the dressing room, the venerable coach John Adams congratulates Broc on the best game he has ever witnessed; Broc is ecstatic.

Keller appears white-faced, shirt ripped open, looking like someone who has suffered his greatest ordeal. The thrill of victory! The Bulldogs are ready to peak.

They have just won the Vincennes Semi-Final, considered by many the toughest of the four held around Indiana. At least *The Evansville Courier* asserts it is in the March 11 edition.

After the memorable showdown, Dan Scism paints this canvas of Broc in his "Sew It Seams" column:

> Jerrel is an individual player. He's individual in the same sense as Red Grange. . . on the gridiron; . . or Joe Gordon was at second base in the 1943 world series. In other words, he has unusual ability as a cage player. He is gifted with a deft touch in tossing a ball through the iron ring. He is quick as a cat with his muscles and even faster, if possible, in his thinking—in sizing up the situation when the storm is at its peak on the floor. . . . There has never been a dribbler and ball handler like him in Evansville that this writer has seen.

So, the Semi-Final nets are snipped by Evansville's Bosse Bulldogs. Final stop? Indianapolis! The IHSAA State Finals. The dream of every Hoosier high school cage player.

Before we go though, a warm story out of the Washington—Bosse Semi-Final game! Although Broc sometimes appears to the competition as a cocksure, self-centered, ball-hogging show-off, in the fourth period—when the outcome is still up in the air—Broc proves a compassionate, respectful, good sport.

With the score close and after a missed Hatchet shot, Gilkinson crashes to the floor. Both teams charge to the other end of the floor. But, Broc eyes Gilkinson still flat on his back in obvious pain. Instead of dribbling down and taking advantage of five on four, Broc dribbles, slows, and glances appealingly at Referee Allen Klinck who whistles play to a halt. Happily, Gilkinson recovers.

Why did the little carrot-top pause? Protocol? Respect? Sportsmanship? You call it.

In winning the Vincennes Semi-Final, Washington's newspaper, with this headline kicker, attributes much of the triumph to Broc:

Jerrel's Brilliant
Playing Had Much
To Do With Victory

So overwhelmed with Broc's play, Associated Press (AP) Sports Editor Jim Mitchell trumpets Broc's exceptional Semi-Final performance.

> Broc Jerrell, the Bulldogs' great guard. . . staved the Hatchets off all evening in one of the greatest individual performances ever seen in the Vincennes semi-final. Jerrel playing despite a broken index finger in his left hand, salted away twenty points. . . . (sic)

To celebrate the victory, school officials promote festivities and a huge bonfire at Enlow Football Stadium adjacent to Bosse. During the frolicking, one beautiful blonde coed pursues teammate after teammate, vying for victory kisses. Succeeding in catching tall Norris Caudell, she must pull his lanky, six foot two inch frame to her level for a kiss.

But, the boy she really seeks to corral is Broc—and she does.

Laurels, too, visit the Bulldogs after the Vincennes Semi-Final. Almost immediately Jack Matthews, Bud Ritter, and Broc Jerrel are posted to the First Team of *The Evansville Courier's* ALL-STAR TEAM. Also named are Washington's Frank Gilkinson and Jack Schiffli. A formidable five!

PART IV

13

TICKETS, PEP, PRECIP

To the future. The Bulldog train now rumbles toward the state capitol. All aboard for *In-di-a-na-po-lis*!

For the State Final, Bosse High School receives only 750 tickets, a slim allotment angering most Bosse boosters since 1500 fans phoned the school's athletic office for tickets. Initially even Coach Keller's mother and sister are denied tickets because they are not regular attenders at Bosse games. If his family doesn't receive them, Coach Keller threatens to steal the tickcts.

Among those who will get in, however, is Bud's uncle, Evansville Mayor Manson Reichert, whose first basksetball game was the Bosse—Washington Semi-Final bout in Vincennes. He liked it immensely, especially "that fellow Jerrel."

One of Mayor Reichert's meetings before the State Final concerns victory celebrations and crowd control in Evansville if the Bulldogs win. It seems IHSAA Commissioner Arthur Trester notified Bosse Principal Carl Eifler that he should make advanced plans to handle "the situation in case Bosse won."

To minimize the possibility of any premature and unruly victory festivities, a spokesman for the Evansville Police Department tells the *Courier* that a mammoth celebration will be held Sunday (the day after the championship game) at 3:00 P.M. if Bosse wins. But the spokesman stipulates that any undue hilarity beforehand will result in arrests. Evansville hopes but braces at the same time; no Evansville city team has ever made it to the State Final evening game.

To send the team off to the State Final, a bona fide full-scale pep rally is held early Friday morning in the Bosse Auditorium.

As a special touch for the assembly, someone suggests "B.B.I.S.C." It seems all through the Semi-Final pep assembly a strange voice from behind the curtain uttered "B.B.S.F.C." The acronym means "Bosse Bulldogs Semi-Final Champs." "B.B.I.S.C." means "Bosse Bulldogs Indiana State Champs." Hope springs eternal.

From all city public and parochial high schools, come cheerleaders, players, coaches, and well-wishers. To a man the team is grateful and encouraged. One memorable chant, comes from

Harp and his Harem
Left to right: Delores Wingfield, Maxine McGowan, Earl Harp, Joyce Glover, Norma Ledgerwood

Evansville's only all black high school, the Lincoln Lions. Their cheer virtually "tears the roof off" the auditorium and provides the most upbeat moment in the rally:

Cheerleaders: "Is the river wide?"
(Evansville sits on the Ohio River)
Fans: "Satisfied!"
Cheerleaders: "Satisfied?"
Fans: "Satisfied!"

Repeated two or three times, the cheer perfectly reflects the relaxed, carefree yet capable and confident attitude of Bud and Broc and of the team in general—a winning attitude. In the words of veteran IHSAA basketball official, Ox Hartley (of poultice fame), the Bulldogs were a "Loosie, goosie bunch of boys—didn't seem they had a nerve in 'em. Couldn't rattle 'em, especially Broc." Highly respected, Mr. Hartley officiates several Bosse basketball games during the 1944 season.

With the assembly over at 10:00 in the morning, the Bulldogs head north to the Fairgrounds Coliseum in Indianapolis.

To organize the cheering, Bosse sends one male and four female cheerleaders. One note before departure, however. In keeping with the superstitious lore already reported, there is a current belief among Evansville fans that now bears mention. On Thursday or Friday before the Sectional, before the Regional, and before the Semi-Final it has rained. On this Friday morning Evansville awakens to the aftermath of a rain storm. Destiny?

14

THE CLUB, SHOWTIME, SCALPERS

When they arrive at the Indianapolis Athletic Club at about 4:00 P.M., Coach Keller tells the boys to prepare for shooting practice shortly. The Club is very accommodating: each boy has his own room; food is bountiful and delectable; staff are kind and helpful. After practice and dinner, McCool, Hollman, Whitehead, and Podjo accompany Dr. Whetstone to the movie *The Purple Heart.*

But, Yonicker, Schmidt, Caudell, Matthews, Bud, and Broc are escorted by the Kilpatrick family to an amateur stage show. Consensus is the show talent is mediocre and that pep assembly skits are funnier. Because team curfew is 10:00 P.M., they leave the show early. On the way back to the Club, some go to the corner drugstore for Ovaltine to help them sleep more soundly. Ovaltine?

All the while, Coach Keller investigates La Porte, getting coaches' tips and any kind of scouting information he can glean.

Of the 778 teams that began the struggle for the State Basketball Crown in the Sectionals back in February, only Anderson, La Porte, Kokomo, and Bosse remain. On that favored Anderson team that received 164 votes is Brooklyn Dodger great-to-be Carl Erskine who plays with all his heart. But, his true championship talent is found on the baseball diamond not on the hardwood.

This year's Final must be played in Indianapolis' Fairgrounds Coliseum because Butler Fieldhouse (for years the site for playoffs) is being used by the Navy in the War Effort.

Almost overwhelmed, the Bulldogs receive their first police escort from the Indianapolis Athletic Club to the Fairgrounds Coliseum. Upon arrival they see disappointed fans standing around each entrance about twenty deep waving large bills for cherished game tickets. For one of the *legitimate* tabs to the State Final game, fans pay A.L. Trester's established gate price of $2.20. But scalpers are getting about forty times that. Business is slow but persistent; reportedly a Kokomo fan paid eighty dollars for one evening session ticket.

The Indianapolis' Fairgrounds Memorial Coliseum itself is a mammoth structure with numerous tall and wide windows all around to capture light. As they trudge through slush from last night's snow-storm up to the unloading zone of the "cowbarn," Coach Kilpatrick asks the boys, "Wouldn't that thing hold a lot of hay?" Some goose pimples and shudders are removed by that rural tension easer.

One major difference between the Coliseum and Butler Fieldhouse could affect a player's perception and performance. Coliseum backboards are not suspended from the roof as in the Field-house. But they are glass in the Coliseum not wooden. So, to become familiar with the boards and their construction before the La Porte bout, the Bulldogs take a few pokes at the basket.

In Indiana, basketball is a passion and proof is visible in the Indianapolis Coliseum. Although the first game doesn't start until 1:30 P.M., by 10:00 A.M. 3000 fans are seated. Also expected are 125 daily newspapers and 13 radio stations. Hoosier Hysteria!

15

KOKOMO "COOKS" INDIANS, LESS REST

In the first afternoon game, the referees are dressed in bright green as Kokomo meets rival Anderson, tourney favorite, in the first game. Following his policy, Coach Keller allows the Bulldogs to watch almost all the contest before dressing for their afternoon game. Know the opposition!

During this game, the most prominent basketball booster in Hoosierdom arrives for roundball festivities—The Honorable Henry F. Schricker, Governor of Indiana.

Lunging to an early 10-4 lead, the Kokomo Wildcats stretch it to 17-5 at half. Not to be squashed, the Anderson Indians gallop to within one, 21-20, at the third quarter stop. And with fewer than five minutes to play, they even lead.

Though the Indians seem hot and ready to race away, behind Big Tom Schwartz Kokomo does not crack. After tying at 26 on Schwartz' shot under, Kokomo glides to victory. Gene Turner's long shot returns the lead to Kokomo with under a minute to play. Seconds from the gun, Charles Farrington's quarter-court one-hander salts away the triumph amidst an hysterical crowd. It's Kokomo vs. La Porte or Bosse. I wonder which.

Playing the second afternoon game gives that game's victors a decided *dis*advantage: like the first game's winners, they must also play the 8:00 P.M. championship game. But, the winner of the second game has 1½-2 hours *less* rest than the winner of the first game. At every level of tournament play, Bosse has had to play the second afternoon game. So, at about 2:45 P.M. Kokomo begins its respite. Yet, simultaneously Bosse begins its afternoon game against La Porte. Oh, well, it's only been that way since the 1920's in tournament play; whoever plays the second game gets less rest.

Here's a great wide angle shot of the Indianapolis Coliseum during the afternoon game between the Anderson Indians and the Kokomo Wildcats. Although the Anderson Indians are the favorites, you know the rest of the story.

Photo Courtesy *Indianapolis Sunday Star*

16

TACTICS, TIES, AWE

In the 2:30 P.M. game, North meets South: the La Porte Slicers (North) are about 300 miles from the Evansville Bosse Bulldogs' house (South), but the competitive edge is not diminished by distance. In fact, much of the thinking is and has been that stronger, better teams reside in the North. Some of that thinking, however, might be lessened after this match.

The two teams do have common ground; like Keller, La Porte Coach Norman Hubner is in his first year at the helm of the Slicers' basketball program.

To prepare to play La Porte, Coach Keller finds that the leading scorer of the conference, Belzowski hits most field goals from about a 90 degree angle to the bucket. Putting lanky, long-

Tip-off of the afternoon game of the 1944 IHSAA State Basketball Tournament in the Indianapolis Coliseum between the La Porte Slicers and the Bosse Bulldogs.

Bud (left) leaps against number 32, Radecki (right).

But, what's Bud doing with his left hand in Radecki's side? Surely he's not pushing off?

Photo Courtesy *AP Wire Service*

armed Caudell on him, Coach Keller feels he can be contained. Each time Belzowski arrives at his favorite shooting position, Caudell is there. He possesses the often uncanny ability to be at the right place when needed. Belzowski tallies only five. The tactic works.

Bud, too, performs especially well in the State Final. After he works himself inside, he has a great hook shot which he often practices. Holding the ball against his chest with one hand, he fakes a shot with the *empty* one; the defense usually leaps six feet in the air while Bud smoothly, effortlessly puts it up. Against La Porte's Radecki, Bud executes the shot flawlessly, drawing two fouls from him and crushing his confidence.

But, before that point the Bulldogs have a rough road.

For uniforms Bosse is clad in red satin, trimmed in gray. Taking the court wearing loud orange uniforms with a black stripe, the La Porte Slicers appear confident, strong, impenetrable.

Continuing a custom begun in early January, just before the game the La Porte team indulge in their unusual good luck ritual. Ten multi-colored Christmas neckties, belonging to the players, are placed one by one around manager Wilbur Frankinberger's neck. And each time the ritual has been performed, the La Porte Slicers have won. Look out, Bulldogs!

17

DELIGHTFUL BULLDOG AFTERNOON

For most of the contest, fans are frenzied. In first quarter action, Bud scores Bosse's first five while Radecki and Banner tally ten for La Porte. Time out Bosse. After the Slicer's Radecki sinks two foul shots on Bud's infraction, La Porte is up 12-5 at the first gun. Uh Oh!

Second quarter, the Bulldogs practice a poor game of catch-up. Fortunately, however, after committing three fouls (two against Bud), Radecki is benched. Then Broc dazzles all by steering through the whole La Porte team to score. The gap is narrowed to 14-10.

Although Slicer scouting chief, Harold Hargrave, told La Porte Coach Norman Hubner his team would face ''one of the best ball handlers in Indiana high school hardwood history in Bosse's

Bryan (Broc) Jerrel, . .'' La Porte seems to shine, actually galloping ahead.

After several field goals (long bombs really) by La Porte's Banner, Belzowski, and Schneider, the Slicers cut out a 22-13 margin. Time out Bosse.

About this time former Bosse basketball great Louis Boink heaves two lucky pennies from his section across the hardwood to the La Porte cheering section. Having received them at the pep rally, he wears them in his shoes all week for good luck.

Because he feels luck has run out of them, he tosses them to La Porte to jinx their hot hitting streak. Apparently the ploy works; La Porte cools off—Bosse heats up! Finally the Bulldogs rebound with two goals from Caudell and Schmidt. Halftime lead by La Porte still a significant 24-17.

The Bulldogs have never been an exceptional afternoon team *nor* a threatening first-half squad. Team members explain they always need to size up their opposition—to determine how hard they have to play to win.

In the locker room Grandpa tells the boys to get out the eraser and wipe out the La Porte lead.

Starting the second half, Broc hits a one-hander; Bud puts back a missed Matthews' free throw and hits a free toss himself to crimp the score. La Porte by two. Time out La Porte. After the break, Broc hits from near the center circle to tie at 24. Painstakingly Bosse slinks away from the Slicers, mostly on charity tosses. Among the foul shots late in the third quarter, Broc's is the most dramatic and memorable; he tells it best:

> I was at the foul line and La Porte fans were right behind our basket. I got ready to shoot and they were waving their arms and pounding the rafters down. I handed the ball back to the official three times before hitting nothing but strings. Next time down the floor I stopped and bowed in the general direction of the La Porte cheering section. When I went back to the line later in the game, you'd have thought you were in a funeral home. They didn't utter a sound.

With grace under pressure! Bosse now by four! The Slicers bag a couple by Wendt and post a free throw. The Bulldogs do much the same.

Remember the tricky out-of-bounds play that Caudell and Matthews pull to get an easy two points. One of the most dramatic and timely illustrations of that deceptive tactic occurs late in the La Porte contest.

Matthews takes the ball out under the Bosse hoop. As he prepares to pass the ball in to Caudell, Caudell wears his most pitiful facial expression and complains in his very convincing acting style, "Hey, I'm supposed to take it out on this play!" At this point the La Porte defender backs off and walks away waiting for Caudell to take the ball out. Then, Matthews flip-passes the leather to Caudell for an easy deuce. Right? Wrong! Caudell *misses* the bunny. Alone. Under. Easy. He misses.

Well, he's so upset at himself—thinking he's let the Bulldogs down—that by quarter's end he's almost sobbing. But, Broc reassures him, his teammates rally around him, and he overcomes it by the beginning of the fourth. Quarter's end, Bosse 32-29.

In the fourth, La Porte vaults back behind Heise's dunk (yes, even in 1944), and Broc hoists another one-hander. Mid quarter, Bosse leads 34-33, never to let up or look back. From a difficult side angle, Caudell bags two; but Rucker responds with a handsome hook. Broc dribbles the side line and lofts another long one.

Fouling out, Caudell is replaced by McCool. With 80 seconds, Bosse leads 38-36. Broc scores the Bulldogs' final three. And with just two seconds Schneider snares La Porte's last two. Final: La Porte Slicers 38, Bosse Bulldogs 41. How sweet it is!

Gliding behind the team toward the dressing room after the victory over La Porte in the second afternoon game, Coach Keller experiences his most thrilling, satisfying moment. For the first time, an Evansville high school team has made it to the State Final final game of the IHSAA Tournament.

While the Bulldogs celebrate in the dressing room, Coach Keller steps outside for a brief respite and inadvertently overhears a nearby phone conversation. The unidentified caller instructs the Kokomo listener how to prepare for the victory celebration: where to make the bonfire, whom to seat on the dais. Kokomo beat the favored Anderson Indians so why not plan the victory? They only need play the Evansville Bosse Bulldogs. The caller confirms Kokomo has it won.

Keller steps back into the dressing room to tell the boys what he's overheard and announce they really needn't play because he's heard Kokomo has it won. The boys are indignant, full of fire. Coach Keller's "mental quirk" at work again.

So awed by the teeming crowd and immense Coliseum, Matthews admits his play against La Porte was negligible. Indeed, after intercepting a pass, dribbling the court's length alone, he missed the bunny. By his own admission he was "scared to death." But the scare only serves to prepare him for the Bulldogs' greatest match-up, their most formidable challenger—the Kokomo Wildcats.

But, they will have additional help in the stands again from ardent Bosse backer, Louis Boink, sitting in Balcony Row *J*. Big Louis Boink tried to scare shots from La Porte in the afternoon and will endeavor to do the same to Kokomo. Every time La Porte shot the ball in the Bosse game Boink let out a scream greater than Tarzan of the Apes. He promises the same yell against the Kokomo Wildcats. Poor Mrs. Boink's ears—and sanity.

In the triumph Broc has 13 of his game high 17 in the final half to spur the fighting Dogs. Dan Scism writes: "Jerrel's handling of the ball, along with his goal sniping, made the Bulldogs look unbeatable. . . ."

Since the Coliseum is ordinarily used for ice hockey games, Dick Anderson pens the following headline twist in his March 19 column:

ALL BROC JERREL
NEEDED WAS PAIR
OF HOCKEY SKATES

He continues with "The Bulldogs, chilly in the opening quarters, rallied with Jerrel as the spearhead." Anderson states Broc would have even given Sonja Henie a run for her money on the ice rink; and ironically, Broc is the shortest and lightest of the forty State Final players.

After that narrow victory over La Porte in the second game, Bosse grapples with the Kokomo Wildcats at 8:00 P.M. for the coveted championship of the IHSAA.

Outside the Coliseum, however, a bizarre story unfolds. The father of Bosse student Maggie Maglaris is solicited for his ticket to the final game that night by a plain clothes detective who touts, "Sell your ticket, Buddy?"

Kiddingly, Sam Maglaris teases, "Yea, for the right price!" In reality, Mr. Maglaris wouldn't sell his token for $1000. But the detective thinks he's serious and hauls him to jail where he spends afternoon and evening, missing the final game. Mr. Maglaris is hot but. . . he spends the evening in jail. How sad it is! He was only kidding.

18

UNIQUE FANS

After the victory at the "ice rink," the Bulldogs return to the Indianapolis Athletic Club for rest and a light dinner. But, I don't imagine anyone actually sleeps too long.

By 7:00 P.M. or so, the boys are already suiting up in the dressing room at the Fairgrounds Coliseum. The moment is at hand. Destiny is at work—at least in one peculiar sense it is. Here's how.

There is one unusual, nameless individual in attendance without a ticket. Among the 11,531 fans in Indianapolis' Fairgrounds Coliseum is a baby in the oldest and most unique infant carrier available. My mother, Broc's sister, Betty attends both the La Porte and the Kokomo games. At this time she has been pregnant with *me* for eight months; I will be born April 20, 1944—in about a month. Although I don't recall cheering and clapping (it was a bit cramped), if I did I cheered the Bulldogs. Destiny.

As the crowd rises for the National Anthem, another peculiar but positive omen unfolds. Trotting to the end of the hardwood, a small mongrel sits at attention on his haunches for most of the National Anthem.

The Anthem nearly completed, however, he cuts loose with a series of howls directed towards each section of the Coliseum.

Because of the interruption, about half the fans have difficulty giving their total attention to the "Star-Spangled Banner." But, with the Anthem ended so are the howls. No one knows just how much bulldog the mongrel has in him; but one wonders if the championship bout begins with a dog, will it end with a Dog. After 32 minutes of play, we'll know.

PART V

19

FIGHTING LIKE WILDCATS AND BULLDOGS

Before 11,531 avid hoopsters, the underdog Bosse Bulldogs take the floor for their greatest adventure. Should they win, that dream of Grandpa's from the middle 1930's will be realized. And Grandpa's prophecy and vision will reach fruition.

For the contest, Kokomo wears bright red with blue trim while Bosse sports gray trimmed in red.

Snaring the opening tip, the crowd-favorite Kokomo Wildcats drive under but miss the lay-up. From the side Caudell drops in Bosse's first two. On a fast break pass from Broc, Matthews scores from close. After a free toss it's Bosse 5-0.

Bolstering Kokomo, Schwartz does connect on a one-hander for the Wildcats' first field goal. After a second by Kokomo, Broc zig-zags through the defense to score under. Bosse 7-4. On a jump ball between Broc and the taller Leslie, Broc opts not to jump but zooms where Leslie tips it. Broc passes it to Bud who is fouled by Schwartz. After several more fouls bagging Bosse a mere two points, Farrington throws in a long one as the quarter closes. Although the malfunctioning scoreboard shows various scores, it's Bosse 9-6.

The second quarter, too, brings Kokomo bad luck early as they miss close-in shots. Bud scores on an out-of-bounds play. But Farrington puts back a rebound. Caudell and Leslie trade baskets; Mathews pops two goals in succession. Bosse 17-10. The score board, however, displays numerous numbers. Then, Kokomo's Turner glides down the side and picks up two under.

The "ball of fire" is not only on the floor. Suddenly, action moves to the bleachers where three fans—one of whom is Grandpa—are forced to find different seats when electrical wires in a control box ignite but are quenched by firemen with fire extinguishers.

At this juncture, the massive electric scoreboard goes screwy, requiring officials announce each score over the Coliseum public address system.

Remember the game in Broc's sophomore year when the Coke vendor shouted "Shoot! Shoot!" Broc does. Well, that lesson pays off. Immediately, Broc contacts the senior referee to learn the official time. For the remainder of the game, Broc and the Bulldogs know how much time remains.

Back to the game! A nice out-of-bounds play tallies two for Caudell; Leslie answers from the side with two. Then, Broc lobs a very long one that hits the rear crescent of the rim, bounces straight up, and drops through. In a scramble Caudell hits from close. After trading some free throws, it's Bosse 23-15. Kokomo timeout.

Then, Bud and Broc fast break. Broc dribbles under fast, puts up a beauty, but tumbles into the padding under the basket. Farrington fires one close. After Broc's charity toss, a gun shot closes the half with the Bulldogs cuddling a comfortable 26-17 lead.

In the third quarter Bosse steamrolls as Broc continues to captivate fans and media with his keen dribbling and floor savvy. As radio broadcaster, Don Burton, states, Jerrel is "one of the finest high school dribblers we've ever seen!"

Second half, Kokomo controls the tip, but the Dogs steal it as Bud works it into Broc who scores. Matthews drives in for a one-hander. Bosse 30, Kokomo 17. Time-out Kokomo. Because of the sizeable lead and team over-confidence, the Bulldogs begin to lose their wide edge. Broc pinpoints the reason: "We went to sleep, and luckily we woke up in time before they left the gym with our silverware."

Deliberately but slowly the tide changes; Kokomo's Schwartz bags two under. Then Leslie hits from the side. Bosse presses. But Farrington drops in a one-hander. Bosse still 30, Kokomo now

24 after a charity toss. Time out Bosse. On a fancy backhand pass from Broc, Bud bags two. The quarter ends—none too soon for the Bulldogs. Bosse 32-24.

As play resumes, Kokomo recovers somewhat, but Bosse is relentless. On guard McFatridge's foul, Bud sinks a freebie; Schwartz uncorks one of his unique one-hand going-away shots to make it 33-26 Bosse. After two Bosse fouls, the Wildcats creep within five. To prevent this surge, the Bulldogs assume a half-stall (no shot unless it's a sure basket) which Kokomo finally breaks. Four minutes from Evansville's first State Championship and five points up, Turner fakes Schmidt and puts up a one-hander, 33-30 Bosse.

Again Bosse stalls and Leslie fouls Broc who tallies one. Then, Schwartz' shot rings true and in an unexplainable flurry Kokomo leads 35-34. Is the Bulldog dream shattered? A proverbial Cat and Dog fight! Two minutes to play.

When Schwartz fouls Bud, Bud is exhausted from the hard afternoon game and decides to shoot the free throw one-handed instead of two-handed. He tells the Good Lord if He will let him make it, he'll never shoot another free throw one-handed. The leather catches only net. 35 all. Faith.

In furious play Caudell sends Bosse up two batting back a rebound; and Schmidt, loose under, takes a pass from Broc (who stole it himself), and grabs his only two as the Bulldogs inch toward victory with just twenty-five seconds.

An informal Bulldog victory celebration

But, during a time-out, Broc glimpses Coliseum officials rolling out the championship trophies and warns the team, "Let's hold on or I see wings on those trophies!"

Finally, with twelve seconds, Matthews and Fisher must jumpball. Although Fisher is considerably taller, Matthews (Duck Foot?) assures Bud, "I'll get it to you somehow!" And somehow—he doesn't even know how—he does. Bud takes it and after a brief stall the gun sounds. Bosse triumphs. Final Bosse 39, Kokomo 35. The starting Bosse five play without substitution to reign victorious.

Satisfied? Satisfied!

20

POST-GAME HOOPLA IS NETLESS

Delirious, fans crowd the hardwood but are met by a ring of firemen, police, and Coliseum officials. Kokomo fans weep openly amidst shrieks of joy and jubilation from Bosse boosters.

A fireman warns Coach Keller not to go onto the playing floor, but Coach Keller shouts back, "It'll take a bigger man than you to keep me off there!"

The Bulldogs embrace as Coach Keller and Coach Kilpatrick gallop onto the floor. Soon Grandpa and several other Bosse boosters are pumping one another's limbs, hugging, celebrating. Crying lustily, Jack Matthews stands near the ten-second line. Arms around Norm McCool, second-stringer Bill Hollman joins in a good sob.

Minutes after the title tilt, Broc ambles toward fans behind one of the baskets to receive an impassioned kiss from a very attractive brunette named June Whetmer; Grandpa manages only a handshake.

After receiving the cumbersome IHSAA championship trophy, Coach Keller holds it high with hands shaking and knees trembling. When he starts to speak, he encounters difficulty. In his elation he experiences a weakness—likely borne of coaching the first State Championship Team from Evansville, Indiana.

But, Coach Keller manages to utter, "I'm the happiest boy in the world!" (Ironically he came to Bosse to coach freshmen with the condition he wouldn't coach varsity.) Then, he embraces all the Bulldogs. Shortly, he rushes to the stands to bestow a kiss on Mrs. Keller.

Bud admits his relief with "I'm glad that one's over!" The only senior, Schmidt admits, "It was my last chance to be on the championship team." A satisfied Matthews shouts, "Boy, I enjoyed this game most of all!" (Quite a contrast to his reaction to the afternoon performance.) And, in a radio interview, Broc explains "I try to sneak around them not drive through them." He did just that—plus, he shot *over* them.

Next, the Bulldogs ask Grandpa to pose with them for the team picture.

KOKOMO HIGH SCHOOL TEAM—Before the agony of defeat

Left to right (front row): Jim Fisher, Robert Lang, Robert Renshaw, Fred Moore, Harry McCool and Coach Ralph M. King

Left to right (back row): Kenneth Craig, student manager; Chap Farrington, Walter McFatridge, Tom Schwartz, Gene Turner and John Leslie. Photo Courtesy *Kokomo Tribune*

Hoopla and hush after the Finals with Wayne Anderson, Broc's uncle, in the bunch

Bulldogs make *V* for victory in locker room after game

Kneeling left to right: Bill Hollman, Norm McCool, Jack Matthews, Broc Jerrel, Don Tilley, Podjo Scholz, Gene Whitehead, Norris Caudell

Standing left to right: Gene Schmidt, Herman Keller, Rush Jerrel, Arvil Kilpatrick, Bud Ritter

Newspapers report that despite their talent and court acuity, after the game the Bulldogs forget to snip the nets from the Coliseum baskets—the first time in tournament history the victor forgets the spoils. Their jubilation overcomes them, reporters speculate. IHSAA officials promise to mail the prized nets within a week.

However, in a directive from Arthur Trester, the four State Final's teams were instructed not to snip the Coliseum nets—conservation for the War Effort.

Who would forget to snip the nets? (Bud has his pocket knife.) The Bulldogs hadn't in their three previous victories in Sectional, Regional, and Semi-Final play. Why now?

In a week, nets arrive at Evansville's Bosse High School.

Back in the locker room, festivities reach an ecstatic pitch. Papa Ritter, Grandpa, and Evansville Mayor Manson Reichert are among many grinning well-wishers. One of the most welcome and special, however, must be Broc's younger brother Gene, another Washington Elementary School cage player of the first magnitude and former Bulldog mascot on Bosse's 1939 Semi-Final team.

EVANSVILLE BOSSE
Season Record (19-7)
1943-44

Evansville Bosse	42	Mount Vernon	21
Evansville Bosse	46	Winslow	32
Evansville Bosse	35	Fort Branch	30
Evansville Bosse	38	Evansville Reitz	36
Evansville Bosse	25	Evansville Memorial	27
Evansville Bosse	36	Evansville Central (OT)	37
Evansville Bosse	35	Huntingburg	36
Evansville Bosse	48	Jeffersonville	39
Evansville Bosse	36	Sullivan	19
Evansville Bosse	29	New Albany	27
Evansville Bosse	37	Princeton	30
Evansville Bosse	32	Jasper	36
Evansville Bosse	46	Evansville Reitz	25
Evansville Bosse	32	Evansville Central	36
Evansville Bosse	27	Boonville	38
Evansville Bosse	28	Vincennes	30
Sectional (Evansville)			
Evansville Bosse	62	Mt. Vernon-Washington Township	20
Evansville Bosse	32	Evansville Reitz	25
Evansville Bosse	49	Lincoln (Evansville)	31
Evansville Bosse	46	Memorial (Evansville)	29
Regional (Evansville)			
Evansville Bosse	38	Dale	22
Evansville Bosse	43	Boonville	35
Semi-Final (Vincennes)			
Evansville Bosse	46	Mooresville	33
Evansville Bosse	40	Washington	34
State Final (Indianapolis Fairgrounds Coliseum)			
Evansville Bosse	41	La Porte	38
Evansville Bosse	39	Kokomo	35

21

EXPERT MEDIA

After some of the smoke and haze of battle clear, *Indianapolis Sunday Star* reporter Albert Bloemker concedes it might be better to give the Bosse Bulldogs the 1945 title by default. (Except for Schmidt, the starting five are juniors.) Of Broc, Bloemker asserts he's almost a one-man team whose dribbling overshadowed all aspects of the tournament.

Veteran coach Glen Curtis of Indiana State College (Larry Bird's alma mater) testifies Broc, the little dynamo, "does things with a basketball" only rarely witnessed in national intercollegiate competiton.

Defeated Kokomo Wildcat mentor, Ralph King, confirms Bosse's victory is attributable to Broc's singular performance and team defensive strength on the boards.

Indeed, the fame of the 1944 State Basketball Champion Bosse Bulldogs and Broc, the diminutive carrot-top, is not regional or state-wide—it is nation wide. Written up in the Indianapolis newspapers; *Chicago Tribune;* Cumberland, Maryland *Evening Times; Denver Post;* and other dailies across America, the Bosse Bulldogs are nearly famous coast to coast.

Despite news of the War Effort, battles, international intrigues, summits, it seems Americans still want to hear and read about their own, their youth, specifically a small red-headed Indiana boy. When the "waterbug among dreadnaughts," as he is once called, demonstrates his dribbling finesse and game control techniques against the Kokomo Wildcats, folks all over the United States immediately become enamored of the "dynamite mite" of Hoosier roundball.

From the pages of the *Chicago Tribune*, we are advised to forget raising the goal from ten to twelve feet because Broc, the smallest competitor in the 1944 Championship at 5-7 and 133 pounds, led the Bosse Bulldogs to the crown of the Hoosier basketball empire. Hooray for the little man!

The *Hammond Times* asks if Broc is the greatest prep player in America. "Will hc be another Johnny Wooden?" questions *Times* sportswriter John Whitaker.

An exceptional player for the Martinsville, Indiana Artesians who won the State Championship in 1927, Wooden, also a National Basketball

Hall of Famer, coached UCLA to an unprecedented ten NCAA Division I Championships from 1964-1975. His reputation is legendary. Word is that Broc is likely a *better* player because of his ball handling and all around floor finesse. Hoosier hoop geniuses both.

From his ''Shootin' the Stars'' column in the *Indianapolis Star,* December 30, 1956, Bob Collins quotes a letter from John Torphy, a former Bedford, Indiana prep player and Indiana University cager. In the letter Torphy asserts that there are fans who think Broc could handle Wooden easily.

> Jerrel really handled that ball. The only two I've seen who could come close to his calibre were Ralph Dorsey who played at Indiana in 1936 and Mickey McGuire of St. John's and Great Lakes.

Near the end of his letter, Torphy boldly claims ''There still are many who believe Jerrel was the finest ball handler in Indiana High School basketball.'' This writer agrees.

In his ''Speculating in Sports'' column in the *Hammond Times,* Whitaker claims Broc overshadows his teammates and competitors in the Indianapolis Coliseum. Old timers declare him the ''dribblingest fool'' to compete in a recent state tourney.

Dan Scism reports that nearly all his media colleagues at the State Final agree Bosse is the best team and Broc the best dribbler.

But Broc doesn't perform behind-the-back dribbles and other maneuvers for which he is famous. Later he reveals that the ball didn't respond and bounce with the sharpness it should have and which it did at the Vincennes Semi-Final. What could he have done on a normal floor?

Tallying 28 points in two State Final games Saturday, the diminutive Bosse junior throws the scorebook at his foes; Broc scores on a variety of shots, showcasing the drive-in type in which he reaches back over his head and hooks the ball—a la Johnny Wooden.

The Speculator (John Whitaker) further attests Broc is the most valuable man to his team

> 'ever witnessed in a Hoosier final.' Ritter, Caudell, Schmidt, and Matthews are sound ball players; but without Broc 'to set' 'em up they would have difficulty winning an average Sectional. Bosse Bulldogs without Broc would be like apple pie without cinnamon or cabbage without corned beef.

Broc dribbles into history on March 18, 1944.

In fact, 26 years later in his March 6, 1970 "Shootin' the Stars" column in the *Indianapolis Star,* Bob Williams calls Broc a " 'Star of Stars'. . .—the Bob Cousy of Indiana's 1940's basketball era."

Lafayette Journal and *Courier* columnist Gordon Graham nearly canonizes Broc as possibly "the outstanding little man of all Hoosier tourney history." He does everything with the ball except drive a railroad spike into it, and his dribbling is astounding and his passing clever and accurate, Graham continues. Bosse owes its victory to the "darting diminutive sorrel top more than to any other one individual."

He dribbles the ball everywhere, Graham adds, except on the shining head of IHSAA chief Arthur Trester. Weaving in and out of impossible situations, Broc changes pace, sets defenses for set-up shots under the goal, and performs all-around astoundingly, Graham summarizes—not soon to be forgotten by 11,531 avid fans.

And needless to say, Broc and the Bulldogs receive yet another accolade: along with Caudell and Ritter, Broc is posted to the distinguished *Indianapolis Sunday Star* newspaper All-Tourney Team. Kokomo's Farrington, Schwartz, and McFatridge are similarly rewarded. Also placed on the prestigious Team are La Porte's Radecki and Anderson's Anderson.

In retrospect, Jim Mitchell, Associated Press Sports Editor, pens these plaudits on Broc:

> The speedy red-head also was the spark that exploded Bosse's fireworks and the crucial points in both games, and his dribbling and ball handling regarded as the best seen in the tourney in many years was demoralizing to the opposition.

A nine year Indianapolis Fairgrounds Coliseum staffer, Herman Leitz offers his all-time All-State State Finals Basketball Team in Carl Wiegman's column in the *Ft. Wayne Journal-Gazette*. Among the 13 players appearing in final games are these:

Forward—Johnny Wooden, Martinsville, 1927
Guard—Broc Jerrel, Evansville Bosse, 1944
Guard—Bobby Plump, Milan, 1954
Guard—Oscar Robertson ("The Big O"),
    Indianapolis Crispus' Attucks, 1956
Guard—Jimmy Rayl, Kokomo, 1959

Of the thirteen, Wiegman offers his pick for the best five:

Forward—Ron Bonham, Muncie Central
Forward—Dee Monroe, Madison
Center—Johnny Wilson, Anderson
Guard—Broc Jerrel, Evansville Bosse
Guard—Oscar Robertson, Ind. Crispus' Attucks

What a line-up! Does Broc deserve to be there? Yes, says Wiegman. "Broc played a heck of a lot of defense. He may not have been the shooter that Rayl was but he was a valuable team man." You're right, Carl.

The Bulldogs are not only winners at Fairgrounds Coliseum but also at the Indianapolis Athletic Club where they've slept, eaten, exercised, relaxed, and practiced since Friday. As they prepare to leave, Mr. Martin, Club Manager, volunteers this praise for the team:

> This is the finest, most sincere, most courteous group of young athletes that it has been my pleasure to entertain since I have been at the club.

What a group! What a team!

PART VI

22

BACK HOME AGAIN

Upon returning Sunday to the ice and cold of Evansville, fan enthusiasm is still much in evidence. At 3:00 P.M. the city fire department's ladder truck ferries the Bulldogs about two miles in parade fashion from the city's North Side to Bosse High School.

To the din of 1500 Bosse boosters and the blaring of the School Song, the team—minus one—trek onto the stage of the Bosse Auditorium. Momentarily, from behind the act curtain staggers Broc, appearing smaller in a large brown overcoat and a brown hat crushed over his red hair. Lugging the huge championship trophy, he stumbles, smiles, and falls into a chair, almost in a faint. Fans roar approval.

On Monday in honor of winning State on Saturday, school is dismissed.

The Bulldogs travel to Louisville, Kentucky to the huge Madrid Nightclub, owned by Bud's uncle. With entertainment by the Jan Garber Orchestra, the boys and their dates celebrate their triumph to the melodies of the Big Band.

When they return to Evansville late that evening, there is a victory bonfire celebration at Bosse's Enlow Field. In attendance are hundreds of students and fans who watch as Coach Keller lights the huge heap.

Coincidentally, the next weekend the same orchestra appears at the Evansville Grand Theater with the Bulldogs again as guests of honor. Recognizing the team, Jan Garber jests, "I've devoted my entire life to following this Bosse basketball team." As Jan Garber plays the boys' favorites, Matthews joins in on the piano with some fancy boogie-woogie of his own making.

By Wednesday, rumors are already running amok that Coach Keller will take another head coaching job and leave Bosse. In an unmistakenly direct statement, Coach Keller puts rumor to rest in Scism's "Sew It Seams" column:

> No. I'm sticking with Bosse. I don't want any head coaching position. I'm not the best coach in the state but I was lucky enough to be coach of the best team in the state.

Victorious, the Bulldogs ride Evansville's ladder truck down Main Street in cold rain but with warm feelings. Slick?

Heroes of the battle at the Indianapolis Coliseum for the 1944 basketball championship celebrate at an assembly in the Bosse High School Auditorium amidst the cheers and roars of over 1500 fans.

Coach Herman Keller lauds the Bulldogs seated behind him as "true champions in every sense of the word."

From left team members are Norris Caudell, Bud Ritter, Gene Schmidt, Podjo Scholz, Gene Whitehead, Don Tilley, Norm McCool, Broc Jerrel, Jack Matthews, Bill Hollman, and assistant coach Arvil Kilpatrick.

Photo Courtesy *Evansville Sunday Courier and Press*

Wednesday night the Bulldogs are invited by Leo Balkin to the Evansville Coliseum for championship wrestling. Topping the professional wrestling bill are Lou "The Great" Plummer and Ray Eckert. The Bulldogs will be seated in a special guest section for the "Main Event."

One of the amenities of winning the State Championship, Matthews learns, is being invited back to Stanley Hall Elementary School to play boogie-woogie on piano in an all-school assembly. Unknown to Matthews, an eleventh grader, is that his future wife, eighth-grader Betty Dale, sits spellbound in the audience. Destiny at work.

Bud and Broc enjoy a more immediate benefit from their accomplishments. At Bosse, they virtually take over Principal Carl Eifler's office. On any given school day from late March to early June, Bud and Broc can be found in Mr. Eifler's office. In his absence one of them sits in his chair, feet on desk, while both mull over "school policy." And they receive no objections from school secretary, Mrs. Babe Matthews—that's Jack Matthews' mother.

As Evansville's first State Champs, banquet invitations seem unending. At one of the many banquets after winning State, the Reverend Zapp asks Matthews to return thanks. "Return thanks for what?" Matthews questions. Someone at the table pipes in "For the food!" So, offering the prayer many of us have mouthed, Matthews recites:

Kennel Club Celebration

Front row: Broc Jerrel, Norm McCool, Jack Matthews, Podjo Scholz, Gene Schmidt
Second row: Fibber McGeehee, Don Tilley, Bud Ritter, Gene Whitehead, Bill Hollman, Norris Caudell
Third row: Max Ritter, Dr. Harry Whetstone, Julius Ritter, Herman Keller, Arvil Kilpatrick, Phil Bevarly, Tiger Ritter
Fourth row: Rush Jerrel, Dan Scism, L.R. McCool, Dick Anderson, Otis Matthews, Bob Gough, Noble Hollman, Alex Jardine, ''Doc'' Hadley.

God is great; God is good.
And we thank Him for this food.
By His Hand we must be fed.
Give us, Lord, our daily bread.
Amen.

Eighteen years later, Matthews becomes a devout Christian, praying weekly for his teammates and coaches.

With the championship trophies in the Citizens National Bank display windows on Main Street, all of Evansville is able to admire them as they shop in the city's hub. Only a block away is Bosse booster and avid fan, Manny Siegel, owner of Siegel's Department Store.

To show his appreciation to the Bulldogs, Manny invites the State Champs to his store to pick out a gift. Most of the squad amble up and down aisles browsing. But, Bud and Broc immediately dash to the sport coat/overcoat/cashmere sweater departments. Just as they are trying on the coats they want, Manny suggests:

> Well, Boys, I'll tell you what you do. Don't make a decision today! But we got a good assortment of ties, socks, and handkerchiefs. Come back.

When they return, Manny has ten small wrapped packages: one contains suspenders, another a handkerchief, some a pair of socks or a tie. Manny catches on.

23

ALMOST THE LAST WORD

Here are two parting glances at Broc, the Brain, the Little Giant.

In a 1971 edition of the magazine *Hoopla,* Dan Scism takes a look at Broc's talents from a distance of some twenty-seven years. From 1926 to 1968, Mr. Scism covered Indiana basketball and State Final tournaments. Of Broc he writes:

> The most valuable high school basketball player I ever saw. . . .
>
> He could dribble and pass the ball behind his back, and between his legs while setting up traps all over the floor. He could propel it forward with one hand teasingly toward a defender and bring it back with the quickness of a snake's tongue. Once on the Central (Gym) floor a defender fell flat on his face making a violent lunge for the ex-

> tended ball. Broc laughed and had to duck a swing when his embarrassed opponent arose.

Evansville Sunday Courier and Press writer, Cliff Guilliams, has this praise for Broc:

> Without question, one of the truly great players who helped make Evansville prep basketball progress through the years is former Bosse sharpshooter Bryan 'Broc' Jerrel, a clever, ball-handling wizard who led the Bulldogs. . . .

The dream that Grandpa, Broc, and the boys hatched in 1936 has become reality.

Yes, as a junior Broc did spearhead the Bosse Bulldogs to the 1944 Championship of the State of Indiana against 777 other schools. The question now is simple: Can he lead them to another championship next year as a senior? Or is this victory just a one-time accidental accomplishment? A fluke?

Except for the graduation of Gene Schmidt, the other starters will be back to defend their title. Rounding out the starters will be one of the original foursome from Washington Elementary School—the very able Norm McCool. For next season, then, Bosse will boast starters McCool, Caudell, Matthews, Bud, and Broc.

Indeed, on the floor of the Indianapolis Fairgrounds Coliseum after winning the IHSAA State Basketball Championship, the Bulldogs shouted, "We'll be back next year!" Hopefully, the littlest champion will return in the same rare, exquisite, and dazzling style to champion the Evansville Bosse Bulldogs to the pinnacle of Hoosierdom's greatest prep tournament for the second straight year. Destiny?

PART VII

24

BROC TIPS AND QUIPS

Here's Broc's best advice—the best from the best.

For any boy or girl athlete to effectively compete in sports, body and mind must be in peak condition.

The body! When young, an athlete's body is often already somewhat conditioned. For getting in better shape, heed the coaches' advice; he knows specifically what he wants his players to do.

Of course, smoking, drinking, chewing tobacco, using drugs or steroids should be shunned.

The mind! Broc states it best: "Between the lines, I just wanted to play. I didn't care about anything else!"

Just getting up in the morning causes some people great pressure and anxiety; learn to make the pressures work *for* you not *against* you. If you want to play roundball, welcome a challenge as an opportunity to excel not fail.

Grandpa possessed an unquenchable desire to succeed, triumph; Broc too. Was it inherited? Was it developed? Was it a combination? Not even a psychiatrist can tell conclusively.

From his understanding, Broc believes a child is *born* with desire. But, it can also be developed—developed especially effectively if success is made. In other words, success breeds desire. The earlier the success, the greater the desire; *and* the sooner it's identified and developed. Most significantly, the smaller the player, the greater the need for desire (*The Little Engine That Could? The Tortoise and the Hare?* David and Goliath?).

The advice seems simplistic, but it isn't. The smaller player must work harder and have greater desire than the taller player because the taller almost always has the edge in getting the nod from the coach to play. Remember Broc is cut from the freshman scrimmage team.

And, without proper instruction in the fundamentals of shooting, dribbling, and passing, there is hardly any future.

While gaining much needed early instruction, it's important to employ an adjustable-height goal or a shorter goal. Goal height should be determined by how smoothly and unforced the beginner lofts the ball. Younger players should not strain to shoot at too high a goal. As with shooting, nearly all aspects of the game should be fluid and smooth, utilizing the whole body not just hands and arms.

Ideally where should that shot originate on the floor? With proper form, of course, the best shot to take is about a twenty-footer at a moderate angle to the basket. But, Broc's keenest advice is "If a guy is closer to the basket and open, throw it to him!" Although no statistics on assists are tallied in 1944, Broc roughly estimates he passed for up to 70 per cent of the team's scoring. And, seldom look where the pass is intended; Broc didn't.

As the young player develops and masters the fundamentals, he must learn to do more. Learn to dribble with either hand for greater and quicker control and less chance of having it stolen. Never watch the dribble; use peripheral vision to watch the other nine players, the clock, the coach.

Master the behind-the-back dribble—it's deceptive and unpredictable. In addition, behind-the-back passing is very useful in wrong-footing the defense. But both dribbling and passing must be *practiced* at length.

Lastly. Never say die! When you give up, you give in. And that is not a winning attitude.

25

BROC PREDICTS

What's the future of basketball?

Had we asked Broc the question several years ago, he would have predicted "the three-point shot." Now it's a staple of the game. And why not? To quote Broc, "A shooter from 25 feet should get more points than a guy dropping it down in!"

To raise or not to raise?

Talk of jacking the goal from 10 feet to 12 has persisted for at least half a century. It's very unlikely the goal will be raised. The reason is quite plausible.

Shorter players would have an even more difficult time heaving the ball to a 12 foot high basket; whereas, taller players would have a greater advantage shooting into a higher basket. The taller player would have an edge the shorter one loses.

At 12 feet the goal is considerably more out of reach to a 6 footer than it is to a 6-7 or 6-11 leaper.

Not to raise.

PART VIII

26

REMEMBERANCE

Year after year, Broc's astounding basketball ability lives in memory, in headlines, and in the accomplishments of the Evansville Bosse Bulldogs. Forty-five seasons after the Bulldogs snare the 1944 Indiana State Championship, this writer encounters a stranger admiring his automobile in an Evansville shopping mall parking lot.

As we chat, Bill Hannah states he hails from La Porte, Indiana. Remembering Bosse beat the La Porte Slicers in the afternoon State Final of the IHSAA tournament in 1944, I counter with, "Up there in Slicer country?"

"Yeah!" he asserts happily.

"I'm writing a book about the Bosse Bulldogs who beat your Slicers in '44," I offer.

"Sure!" he responds, "I used to love to come to Evansville to watch Broc Jerrel and Bud Ritter play basketball."

Well, I learn Bill Hannah was Arvil Kilpatrick's assistant coach at small Mackey High School, 17 miles north of Evansville. Though 72, Bill still remembers Bud and Broc as if they played last week. Fame.

Almost monthly somewhere in Indiana someone writes an article about or makes a reference to Broc and the Bulldogs—more often during basketball season. Newspaper headlines crop up with surprising frequency: *The Indianapolis News,* Sunday January 30, 1988. Byline Wendell Trogdon. Headline: " 'Broc' Jerrel inspired short players to new heights."

According to Trogdon, Broc

> could dribble the ball like a magician and shoot like a marksman. He used brashness and craftiness to offset his height. . . .
>
> He had become the instant hero to thousands of kids the previous March (winning the state title). . . .
>
> Anyone who wasn't bigger than 5 feet 8, declared himself 'Broc' in pickup games and tried to emulate the way the (radio) announcer said Jerrel played.

Pick up any Indiana newspaper during basketball season and you might just find an article lauding the amazing talents of Bryan "Broc" Jerrel and the Evansville Bosse Bulldogs. Destiny.

27

DESTINY

A team that constantly triumphs against stacked odds, the Bosse Bulldogs, I am more and more convinced, are a team of Destiny—they are supposed to win! Don't get me wrong. Destiny doesn't win games—talent and perseverance do. But the team was destined to have the talent (nurtured by Grandpa, the coaches, and practice) and the never-say-die attitude.

Despite that attitude, they often lose in regular season (seven games). But not because they quit or are incapable. During regular season they're hardly ever at full strength because of illness or injury. In tournament play they never lose, but then after Sectionals begin hardly anyone is ill or injured—except Bud and Broc. Destiny?

That's the difference! Because it is their Destiny, they are champions. But, will they be able to overcome even greater odds next season—Coach Keller's nearly fatal bleeding ulcer, devastating flooding from the unbridled Ohio River, and relentless opponents striving to dethrone them.

But, that's *another* story.

Destiny?

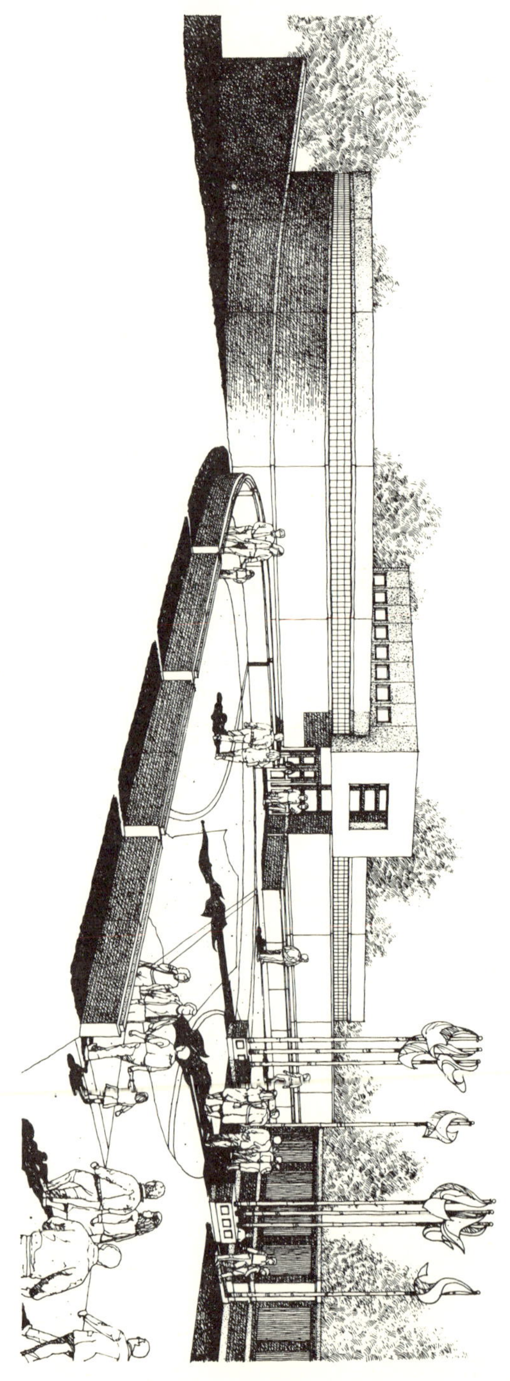

THE NEW INDIANA BASKETBALL HALL OF FAME, NEW CASTLE

The final accolade to be heaped on the 1944 Bosse Bulldogs comes as Coach Herman Keller and four of the starting five are inducted into the prestigious Indiana Basketball Hall of Fame.

In 1968, Keller is inducted. Bud is brought in in 1975. Broc is initiated in 1976. Caudell receives his induction in 1985. Schmidt is bestowed the honor in 1987.

It would seem very appropriate to this writer that the final member of the starting five, Jack Matthews, be inducted into the Hall of Fame just as soon as the electors can bring it about. Only then will the circle be fully drawn and the greatness of the total team be recognized.

All are Hall of Famers.

Benjamin Bosse High School

Location: Southwestern tip of Indiana in Evansville

Named: In honor of Evansville mayor, Benjamin Bosse

Opened: 1924

School Colors: Scarlet and Gray

Mascot: Bulldog

School Song: Sung to tune of *Illinois Loyalty*

We're cheering for you, Bosse High;
We're loyal to you, Bosse High.
We'll back you to stand
'Gainst the best in the land,
For we know you have sand,
Bosse High. RAH! RAH!
So fight to the end, Bosse High;
Go crashing ahead, Bosse High.
For our team must be the winner;
Fight, Boys, for we expect
A victory from you,
Bosse High.

If you would like to send a copy or copies to others, please fill out the form below and send the proper postage and payment. List additional names & addresses on back. Please allow 6 weeks for delivery.

Please send ________ copies of *BROC: THE LITTLEST CHAMPION* to:

Name ____

Street Address ____________________________________

City ______________________ State ___________ Zip ___________

BROC: THE LITTLEST CHAMPION — $9.95

Tax, Postage, Handling — $1.00

Total Cost — $10.95

Amount Enclosed ___________

Please make checks payable to:
Timothy Baize

Mail orders to:

TIMOTHY BAIZE
2305 Glenn Avenue
Evansville, Indiana 47711